RECIPES
from a
GREEK ISLAND

RECIPES
from a
GREEK ISLAND

SUSIE JACOBS

Special photography by
Linda Burgess

CONRAN OCTOPUS

FOR MY MOTHER IN MEMORY OF HER MOTHER

First published in 1991 by
Conran Octopus Limited
37 Shelton Street
London WC2H 9HN

This paperback edition published in 1993 by
Conran Octopus Limited

Reprinted 1995

In the transliteration of the Greek language in this
book, the Greek letter delta is represented by 'th', rather
than 'd', which may also be seen.

Both metric and imperial quantities are given in
the recipes. Use either metric or all imperial, as the two
are not interchangeable.

Art Editor – Helen Lewis
Project Editor – Denise Bates
Editor – Pepita Aris
Designer – Christine Wood
Picture Research – Nadine Bazar, Abigail Ahern
Production – Julia Golding
Home Economists – Jane Suthering (photography)
Valerie Eames (recipe testing)
Photographic Stylist – Debbie Patterson
Painted Signs – Barbara Mullarney Wright
Illustrations – Sarah Venus

British Library Cataloguing in Publication Data
Jacobs, Susie
Recipes from a Greek Island
I. Greece, Cookery
I. Title
641.509495

ISBN 1 85029 803 3

Typeset by Facet North, Leeds
Printed in Hong Kong

CONTENTS

INTRODUCTION

THIS BOOK IS THE RESULT of living and cooking on a Greek island for fifteen years. As I write this, I look out of my window, past the winter jasmine climbing up the pergola, over to the hillside opposite. The sun casts patterns across a small herd of sheep grazing around a cypress tree. There is no intruding sound of cars – transportation here is by foot or donkey only. There is little in the way of modern means of communication or entertainment.

We read the Herald Tribune one day late, which is enough to keep us in touch with important events and sparse enough to prevent nonsensical, non-news from cluttering our minds. There is always the radio for fresher news.

During the summer months, the movies shown in the little outdoor cinema change every night. Cats come and go across the wall which is the screen, indifferent to the ghostly images moving below them. As the season advances, so the geraniums grow higher into the screen. Then the movies are silenced for yet another year. But the cats still come and go, the geraniums continue to grow.

Happily, friends come and go too during every season and there are always books, music, swimming, long walks and convivial, unhurried meals. We live in a 200-year-old house that is more demanding than a jealous lover. It takes blind devotion and inordinate time just to maintain a comfortable level of gentle decay. Slowly, slowly more trees are planted, gardens expanded and animals added to the slightly chaotic menagerie. A working farmlet is on my 'list of things to do if I live long enough', which also includes winemaking, distilling, pressing my own olives, and so on, *ad infinitum* . . .

One is cast upon these shores and cast upon oneself to create a life and a cuisine out of the simple resources at hand and in the heart. The beautiful, rock-bristling, almost forbidding landscape bears the olive, almond, fig, carob,

caper – uncountable wild things; it harbours goats and sheep; our thirsty, sun-drenched gardens produce a wealth of fruit and vegetables – lemons and oranges, tangerines and quinces, grapes and loquats, artichokes and garlic, peppers and courgettes, tomatoes and aubergines. The surrounding sea no longer teems with fish but still provides us with an adequate array of Mediterranean catch – spiny lobsters, octopus, squid, red mullet, needle fish, rockfish, sea bass, sea bream, picarel, bogue, grouper, various eels, sea urchins and an occasional tuna, shark or hake.

Across the narrow strait which divides Hydra from the Peloponnese come local merchants, their *caïques* laden with fresh produce, highly prized semolina flour, village-made sausages and yogurt, young beef and freshly pressed olive oil. And across the sea and skies come friends bearing fresh ginger, eau de vie, vanilla beans, Chinese sesame oil, Indian rice, Thai lemon grass and galingale, Russian caviar, Swiss morels and American maple syrup. It is as if all the ancient spice routes led straight to our door.

At a time when awareness of the landscape is receding deeper into the collective unconscious, under a thickening layer of concrete and technology, this island which looks from a distance like a forsaken, grey rock rising from the sea, unfolds to offer us a life of simple pleasures and rough-hewn grace. I wish you could see the tiny wild cyclamen softly pushing their pink blossoms through limestone fissures and smell the lemon blossom in spring. They are the sights and smells of Greece.

I aim to share with you some of the recipes which have been inspired by the bounty of this landscape, hoping they evoke a sense of place and season and reflect the unchanging Greek sensibilities towards food, eating and good health. Plutarch believed that meat should be used as a support to diet. He said that we should 'eat other foods more in accord with nature and less dulling

to reason, which is kindled from plain and light substances... For the earth yields in abundance many things not only for nourishment, but for comfort and enjoyment.'

Some of the recipes in this book have been taught to me by friends and neighbours. Some have been described by people recalling the cooking of their mothers and grandmothers. They are much richer in tradition than most of the loveless food you will find in today's tourist tavernas.

I am not a scholar, but for food's sake I read everything from Homer and Hesiod to recipes on the sides of boxes. All of this information sinks into my brain, resurfacing as a recipe. I make no attempt at orthodoxy. Whether it started as an Indian *tarka* or an Egyptian *takla*, a Russian *pirozhka*, or a Greek *pítta*, the result may be a mongrel, but it is nevertheless an interesting and pleasing dish. From my haphazard research it is clear to me that there is a culinary silk road that has yet to be fully explored historically and anthropologically. I don't believe that any of the

MENDING NETS *Fishermen work on their nets in the lengthening rays of the afternoon sun.*

recipes in this book veer off the path leading around the Mediterranean basin.

I hope I am able to communicate to you what a great joy it is to me to walk down the 365 stone steps winding to the port, to see what the fishermen have brought in that morning; to stroll around the open market smelling and looking through the stalls for the freshest produce on offer; to climb up the mountain in the afternoon to pick wild greens; to add to a dish some poetic touch from the ancient spice route; and to serve a fresh and honest meal shared by friends and loved ones.

INGREDIENTS FROM A GREEK KELLÁRI

ALMONDS AND WALNUTS

Amýgthala and *karíthia* both probably originated in Asia Minor, but they have been growing in Greece for so long that the Romans called the almond 'Greek nut' and the Persians used the same phrase for the walnut.

A list of their uses could be as long as their years under cultivation! They are ubiquitous in sweets, and not uncommon in savouries, as in *scorthaliá*, the famous almond-and-garlic sauce on page 79. In the north of the country a succulent stew is made with walnuts.

Be careful where and how you buy and store nuts, as a single rancid one can spoil an entire dish. Buy where there is a fast turnover, and refrigerate or freeze them, if you don't intend to use them immediately.

BASIL

Vasilikós, basil, means kingly and basil was associated in ancient rites with love and death. Classical and Byzantine Greeks savoured it, but today luscious pots of basil adorn Greek windowsills to ward off flies and mosquitos. I doubt its efficacy. Some people believe dried basil can be resuscitated by soaking in hot water. I would resort to this only in sheer desperation.

BAY LEAF OR LAUREL

The winning athletes at the first Olympic games were crowned with *dáphne* wreaths, and the Delphic oracle may well have sat over the smoke of smouldering *dáphne* leaves before uttering her predictions. It is equally distinguished in the kitchen.

Elizabeth David advises that dried bay leaves be broken up to extract maximum flavour. If you have a suitable site, a bay tree is not only useful but decorative.

BEANS AND DRIED PEAS

Óspria includes all beans, peas, lentils, chickpeas and broad beans and a wide selection is enjoyed in Greece, such as *fasolákia*, white beans. The small size, haricot, are often used in salads, the medium size, cannellini, in the famous *fasolátha* soup and *gigantes*, butter or lima beans, are made into hearty stews with lots of onions, tomatoes and herbs. The green or brown lentil comes in two sizes, tiny and small, and both become pink lentils when skinned and split. Chickpeas are made into soups and mixed with rice and other grains and are a fast-day staple. Yellow split peas are often made into dips.

Broad beans, *koukía*, are often called fava beans in America: not to be confused with Greek *fáva*, which are yellow split peas. Pythagoras prohibited their use by his followers, as he believed they contained the souls of the dead, but they are nevertheless a staple in the Mediterranean and North Africa. Eaten fresh in spring, and dried, you will find the latter in Middle Eastern groceries.

There is one point concerning *óspria* on which all Greeks agree – they must be cooked in rain water. As most of us in the modern world don't have cisterns in which to collect rain water, soft tap water has to do. Your grandchildren will have grandchildren and the beans still won't have softened if you cook them in hard tap water or salt them before they are done. If your tap water is hard, either use bottled water or put a pinch of baking soda – no more than ⅛th teaspoon to minimize vitamin loss – into the first boiling water. Soaking, of course, is the key to softening pulses and decreasing their cooking time.

BITTER ORANGE

The bitter or Seville orange, *nerántzia*, is probably the grandmother of sweet oranges, all of which originated in China, and didn't reach the Mediterranean until after Christianity. It is not an eating orange, but lends a flowery tartness to many dishes – and its characteristic bitterness to marmalade. If you can't find them, use half lemon, half orange, or one third of these, with grapefruit.

BREAD RUSKS

If you serve only good bread, and never eat it stale, then here is what to do with that left over. Just cut it into rough slices and bake it in the oven at 130°C (250°F, gas ½) for 45-60 minutes, until all the moisture has evaporated, but the rusks haven't petrified. If they give a little to the touch, they will be hard by the time they cool. You will find them indispensable in cooking.

In Greece these *paximáthia* are made from country bread, full of anise and coriander seeds. They are a Greek staple. They keep forever, are dunked daily into tea and coffee, made into breadcrumbs and served at wakes.

CAPERS

Capers, *kápari*, are the pickled bud of a shrub, native to the Mediterranean and North Africa and growing right out of the stone walls of our house, threatening their collapse. We pickle them out of preference and self-defence – both the buds and the young leaves, which are wonderful in or as salad. Most supermarkets stock capers.

CELERY

The so-called Italian celery, *sélino*, used in Greece looks more like large flat-leaved parsley and it is the wild version of a vegetable that is now cultivated for its stalks. It is not eaten raw, but is used as a herb in many Greek dishes. It is more pungent and flavourful than the cultivated plant, whose slender tops and leaves are the best substitute. In Greece it is cultivated, too, and is easy to grow. Lovage is a good substitute.

CHEESE

When I first came to Greece I was not impressed by the cheeses. They seemed quite ordinary, erratic in taste, texture and quality, but they always tasted of the goat's or sheep's milk, and so of the wild places they had grazed.

Over the years I have come to cherish those qualities. Elsewhere, while mass production has transformed what used to be honest cheese into tasteless rubber, Greek cheeses remain straight-forward, made in the old, unpredictable but authentic ways. Many of the best cheeses are generally not available outside their villages, but here are some of the main ones.

It is redundant to ask for a slice of *féta*, as it literally means a slice in Greek. A basket of bread, a plate of olives and a slice of a 'slice' must be the most common culinary sight in Greece.

Féta is always made from sheep's or goat's milk, a fresh white curd cheese, which may be soft, medium or hard when sold. It is pickled, that is, soaked in a brine so salty that it stops all ripening or ageing. If it is too salty (often the case with imported, commercial *féta*), soak it in cold water for 24 hours. It may be stored like this for up to 10 days – when it may need salt adding back to it.

Graviéra is a Greek version of Gruyère, made from sheep's milk in roughly the same manner as Gruyère, though the resemblance stops there. Uncomplicated and old-fashioned, it is good with fruit.

Kasséri is made from goat's milk, by a process similar to cheddar, and has a smooth texture and taste. It is good as it is, or fried as *saganáki*. Dust a 1 cm (½ in) slice with flour on both sides, fry in hot olive oil and serve with a liberal squeeze of lemon.

Kefalotýri or *kefalograviéra* is a hard cheese, commonly used for grating, made from goat's milk. At its worst, it tastes like salty soap and at its best it is like a good earthy Sardinian *sardo*. It makes great *pesto*, pounded with basil.

Manoúri and *anthotýri* are a pair of creamy cheeses from ewe's milk, which are used to make cheesecake, or are served with fruit or honey. When salted, however, they are eaten plain, dressed like *féta* or are used for cooking. Try them if you have the opportunity!

Mizíthra is a whey cheese like Italian ricotta. Fresh and unsalted it is used in the cheesecake *siphnópitta* (*see page 128*). The top quality ones are good eaten plain with a drizzle of honey. But they are also salted, dried, covered in wax for storage, then used for grating. Dried *mizíthra* can be soaked in a bowl of water, though it will never resemble its fresh self. It is low fat cheese which is worth searching out.

CINNAMON AND CLOVES

Along with the pepper and nutmeg *kanélla* and *garíphalla* are the commonly used 'spices of Araby', so called because the trade was dominated for centuries by the Arabs, back to the time of Herodotus, who wrote nearly 2,500 years ago of man-eating birds on nests of cinnamon bark.

At one time these spices were prohibitively expensive. Today you will find a stick of cinnamon in the remotest shepherd's hut.

I highly recommend that you grind your own spices. An electric coffee grinder is superb: throw in a handful of rice to clear away the residue of the last spice.

COFFEE

When I first came to the islands, I was told that the Greeks were great connoisseurs, and some could even tell from which spring a glass of water had bubbled forth. With my mouth full of bitter coffee grounds, I wondered why they were so passionate about their coffee. Until I reached for the glass of water that is always served with it. Then I realized that the coffee made the water taste better.

Since then, I have learned to wait for the grounds to settle and prefer Greek (more accurately Turkish) coffee. It is made from beans that are ground to a fine powder in a tiny pot, a *bríki*, which looks like something that should be used to melt butter. The general rule is one teaspoon of coffee to one demi-tasse of water and no sugar for a plain *skéto*, one sugar for a medium *métrio*, and two sugars for a sweet *glykó*.

CORIANDER

Kolíandron, is native to the eastern Mediterranean and India. Both the seeds and green leaf are used, the latter sometimes called Chinese parsley. In Greece the seeds are used in pickling, baking, seasoning sausages and in stews, the leaves in salads and garnishes.

CORN (MAIZE) MEAL

This yellow flour, whose Greek name *aravósitos* means Arab wheat, is ground from American Indian corn (maize) which must have been introduced by the Arabs. They received it from Spaniards returning from America. Like Italian polenta, it comes in coarse or fine textures. It is *not* corn starch which is sometimes, confusingly, called corn flour. Corn meal is a traditional ingredient in country bread and cakes.

CRACKED WHEAT

For a millennium this *pligoúri* was the rice of the poor. Also called burghul and bulgar, it is sold in health food stores. As it is boiled to make it, it needs only a brief soak before it is edible.

CUMIN

A fruit that looks like a seed, *kímino* is a native of the eastern Mediterranean. It is mostly used in Greece for meat dishes of oriental origin.

DILL

In ancient times *ánithos* was also the name for anise, of the same *Umbelliferae* family and now called *glykániso* or sweet dill. The ancients used dill for cooking and for its medicinal properties.

FENNEL

Fennel or *márathos* was found growing wild at ancient Marathon, after which the long distance track event is named. The fronds, stalk and seeds are used for cooking and medicinal purposes. The fronds sometimes replace dill in pickles in my house.

FIGS

Athenaeus, in the 3rd century AD, tells us that the King of India, Bindusara, ordered figs, *sýka*, grape syrup and a philosopher from the Greeks. The produce was duly shipped, but he was informed that trading in philosophers was illegal. As there are over 600 varieties of fig in the world, I wouldn't begin to recommend other than your own choice from those available. They should be firm, neither hard nor mushy, and fragrant.

FILO PASTRY

Fýllo, fine tissues of wheat pastry, are available at some supermarkets and any Greek or Middle Eastern grocery. They come in packets of 12 or 24 sheets, and are 30 cm (12 in) square or 50 x 30 cm (20 x 12 in). They can be stored in the freezer, but must be used soon after defrosting, which should be done slowly in the package. The sheets dry out and become brittle when exposed to the air, so you must learn to work fast and keep those you are not working with under a lightly-dampened towel.

FISH ROES

Taramá, which looks like a kind of paste, is the salted roe of one species of grey mullet. But in these days of dwindling Mediterranean fish, the original is expensive and it is more likely to come from the roe of North Sea cod, carp or tuna. It is most frequently used to make *taramosaláta* and *taramakeftéthes*. Salted or smoked cod's roe can be substituted. This is sold in its skin (which must be removed) in many fishmongers, and also canned.

Avgotáraho, called *boutargue* in France and *botargo* in Italy, is a preparation of grey mullet eggs. The entire egg sack is salted, dried, lightly smoked and coated in a thin layer of beeswax for protection. Locally it is eaten with bread, sliced and drizzled with lemon. It becomes difficult to find commercially. Claudia Roden in her *New Book of Middle Eastern Food* gives instructions for preparing it from whole cod's roe sacks.

The old way of making *taramosaláta* was by grating and pounding *avgotáraho*. Nowadays the easier and more widespread method is to use *taramá*.

There are no salmon in Greece, but *brik*, red caviar or salmon roe, is imported in huge quantities. It comes lightly salted in jars. In Athens one finds colourful fresh pyramids of it on sale, into which I have often been tempted to take a headlong dive.

GARLIC, LEEKS AND ONIONS

From the same *Allium* family, *scórtho*, *prássa* and *kremíthia* all grow wild in Greece. All have lent their lively tastes to Greek cooking for all time. If you have never tasted fresh garlic, pop a few sprouted cloves into a pot or into your garden. They are so sweet and mild, you will be tempted to eat them raw.

I pick wild leek flowers and toss them into the salad in spring — tiny white starbursts that pack a wallop.

GERANIUMS

Scented or 'rose' geranium leaves, *arbaróriza*, are commonly used to flavour jams and jellies, and make a refreshing tea. If you can't buy them at a herbalist or health food store, they are very easy to grow — and almost indestructible. A pot stands in almost every island courtyard, where it is constantly sniffed, fondled and loved by all.

GOAT'S MILK

Goat's milk, *gála katsikísio*, has more protein, less cholesterol and more vitamins than whole cow's milk. It is available at health food stores and some supermarkets. Many people who are allergic to cow's milk can tolerate that of goats. It has been a staple in Greece (and the Middle East) since the neolithic revolution and adds character and flavour to soups and sauces.

GRAPES AND RAISINS

By the first century BC, special varieties of table and raisin grapes, *staphýlia*, had been developed in Greece — and now there are about 8,000 varieties worldwide. The juice of sour grapes was

ONIONS

used to add an acid tang to food before the introduction of the lemon and bitter orange.

A grape vine growing up a garden pergola is a common sight in Greece. I have even seen a few on apartment balconies in Athens. Personally I look forward to the late summer, when I muster my courage and wiles to pick the luscious bronzed berries, while the wasps are not looking. Aside from being eaten fresh, they are preserved in syrup, to be served as a 'spoon sweet'.

The three major raisin grapes all grow in Greece. Thompson seedless provides the golden sultana, the currant is named after Corinth; and the third is my favourite, the muscat grape.

GRAPE LEAVES

Vine leaves, *klimatóphylla*, are used as a handy culinary packaging in Greece, and all the neighbouring parts of the Mediterranean and the USSR too – all places Dionysus is reputed in the myths to have introduced it.

Anything can be wrapped in a vine leaf. They are sold in brine, bottled or in plastic packs, in some supermarkets and Greek or Middle Eastern groceries. Always rinse them before using. If you have a grape vine, pick the tender first leaves. Remove the tough parts of the stems, place the leaves in a colander or sieve and steam them for about 5 minutes. Use them immediately, or pack in sterilized jars with salt brine or vinegar.

GRAPE MUST AND SYRUP

Grape must, *moústos*, is the juice of wine grapes at the beginning stage in the process of becoming wine. 4 kg (9 lb) grapes yields about 1 litre (2 pt) of *moústos*. The grapes are crushed in a large wooden trough or ceramic bowl (hands or a potato masher serve), then are strained through fine muslin, squeezing out as much juice as possible. The muslin should be left to hang over the juice for a few hours.

A traditional and ancient sweet called *moustalevriá* is made every autumn by cooking *moústos* with semolina flour until it is thick enough to be moulded. It is sprinkled with nuts and sesame seeds and served to celebrate the harvest, or is dried in the sun and packed away in tins for later. I believe these dried must cakes were an ancient form of leavening.

Moústos can be cooked down to a thick honey-like syrup, and used as a sweetener – as it was before the introduction of sugar to the western world. This is called *petimézi* in Greek and *vino cotto* in Italian and can be found in the respective groceries.

HONEY

Honey, *méli*, has been the sacred sweetener of most civilizations. Even Aristotle, the father of the physical sciences, couldn't tell what was the nature of the bees' work and hypothesized that honey was collected from the morning dew that fell from the heavens.

Greek thyme honey was most highly prized all over the ancient world. The same Hymettus honey is still sold in Greek grocers. Look also for single source, and herb and flower honeys.

LEMON

Lemónia are relative newcomers to the Greek kitchen – probably less than a thousand years ago. Now nearly every islander has at least one tree, from which they pluck lemons daily to use on, or in, just about everything.

The first lemons in winter are like golden baubles, glistening with their own oil and bursting with perfumed juices. The lucky owners of a tree can pick each fruit with a bit of branch and leaves attached. By doing so, the lemon is tricked into thinking it hasn't been picked and it stays fresh for three weeks. They also look beautiful piled in a bowl in this way.

Wherever lemon leaves are called for in the recipes they are used to line the bottom of a baking or braising pan so that whatever you are preparing is not scorched or discoloured by direct contact with the pan. My attitude is that while you are at it, you might as well include some poetry from the scent of citrus leaves, which are just outside the door of almost any island house, and add a lively perfume to whatever you may be cooking. Substitute them with cabbage leaves, lettuce leaves, vine leaves or scented geranium leaves. If you don't want to lose the subtle citrus perfume by using a more prosaic cabbage leaf, add a strip or two of lemon zest. I put lemon leaves in the Christmas pudding water, or boil them on their own when I want the kitchen to smell like a sunny lemon grove.

LEMON VERBENA

Louísa was introduced to Greece in the 18th century from South America. It immediately became highly prized for the sweet, citrus flavour it added to tisanes and sweets. It is *Lippia citriodoro*, a purple-flowered wall climber, not to be confused with the herb verbena.

Lemon verbena is sold by herbalists and in health food stores. An infusion of lemon verbena with lime flowers and scented geranium makes a good tea – hot or cold – or a good liquid for stewing dried fruits.

LIME FLOWERS

Tílio is widely used as a tisane, appreciated for its soothing flowery taste and effect. In Greece these lime flowers are available at every *bakáliko* or grocery. Look for them in health food stores.

MASTIC

Mastíhi is a resinous gum produced by a shrub, *Pistacia lentiscus*, that grows on the island of Chios. You can find it in Greek or Middle Eastern groceries – little resinous rocks, packed in small plastic boxes. Powdered with pestle and mortar, it is used to flavour sweets and stews with a resinated anise taste.

In the days of the Ottoman Empire, the ladies of the Sultan's harem not only used it as chewing gum, to sweeten the breath and clean the teeth, but also owned the exclusive right to sell all the mastic of Chios, which provided their pocket money. It is a sugar-free, non-chemical chewing gum – the original one, in fact!

The powder is also used to flavour a liqueur called mastíha.

MINT

Thiósmos is spearmint and is widely used in cooking. *Mínthe* is peppermint, and is only used as a tisane. It was the name of a nymph who caught the eye of Hades, King of the Underworld. Due to the jealousy of his queen, Persephone, she was transformed into a plant – remembered in the fragrance released from a patch of wild mint, or of a few leaves between the fingers. Mint is passable dried, but preferable fresh.

OKRA

Okra or ladies' fingers, *bámies*, are widely ignored except in parts of the Mediterranean, the southern US and the Third World. Okra is not, in fact, a vegetable, but an unripe seed pod, related to the hibiscus flower. It is appreciated for its tart, slightly acrid taste and its sticky juices, which have thickened many a stew.

If you can't abide a slippery texture, cut away the stem without opening the pod. Soak the okra in half a cup of vinegar, with a little salt, in a shallow dish in the sun for two hours. Rinse and dry well.

OLIVE OIL

The olive thrives on Greek soil, which has never been ideal for pasturage or major cereal crops. Athenian oil was considered the best in the ancient world and Greece has always traded oil for wheat. As a staple, oil, *elaiólatho*, has always provided necessary calories and vitamins in a simple diet. Today we know that it is a mono-unsaturated fat, that is believed to help the human body metabolize 'bad' cholesterol. However, most of us don't need the extra calories these days, so I have cut the amounts of oil used in the recipes to what I consider a minimum, without sacrificing taste.

My friend Nick, an agronomist, recommends a naturally pressed oil, from the first pressing called 'extra virgin'. This is not refined, and has no refined oil added. The best oils should have low acidity – below 1% – and a clean appealing smell. Virgin and refined oils are also sold mixed – the quality commonly used for cooking.

I have used only olive oil in these recipes, as the other traditional cooking fats, rendered sheep's fat and sheep's butter, are difficult to find outside Greece. As the price of olive oil rises, modern Greece has, of course, switched part of its allegiance to other oils, and to margarine.

OLIVES

Over millennia a great variety of *eliés* has been developed in Greece to suit the climates of particular regions.

Throúmbes are not a variety of olive, but a way of preparation. These olives are salty, wrinkled and black, because they have been left on the branches to wither and fall. Great nets are spread out about the trees and the pickers beat the branches with poles until all the olives have fallen. The olives are put out to dry for a few days and then packed in rock salt. They are ready to eat within a few weeks, or can remain until the next crop appears. Look for them in Greek or

Middle Eastern grocers and be sure to rinse all the excess salt off thoroughly before using them.

Kalamáta olives, which you can find loose or canned in brine or oil are tear-shaped fruit: green, purple or black, depending on the stage of ripeness at which they were picked. They are slit and soaked in often-changed fresh water for ten days, to remove the bitter glucoside. Then they are packed in brine salty enough to float an egg, or in a mixture of two parts olive oil to one part wine vinegar, with various condiments: lemon peel, red chillies, rosemary, thyme, oregano or bay leaf. Now if you have an olive tree, you know what to do with those olives that usually fall all over your garden!

ORANGE FLOWER AND ROSE WATERS

Rothónero and *anthónero* are dilutions of orange flower or rose petal essences. They are used most often, though not exclusively, in sweets.

One whiff will transport you far away to an oriental time and place – which is why I put rosewater in my steam iron.

OREGANO AND MARJORAM

Respectively these herbs are *Origanum vulgare* and *O. marjorana*, so closely related that spice merchants and even a good botanist might have problems telling them apart, once they are dried and crushed. Generally, oregano, *rígani*, is tangier with a more pronounced flavour than marjoram, *mantzourána*. They have both been appreciated since ancient times, and wild Greek oregano is exported dried.

PARSLEY

The warriors of Homer's *Iliad* fed flat-leaved parsley to their horses, and crowned their brave with this common, much-used herb. Sadly, flat leaf parsley is less common in Britain and the US than the decorative curly type.

If I had to choose one herb for all reasons and seasons, it would be this one. Once you have tasted this ancient variety, you will find it indispensable. It is becoming more commonly available at greengrocers and markets and is easy to grow. It is sometimes known as Italian parsley.

RICE

Although rice was first seen in Greece in the 3rd century BC, it remained an expensive delicacy for centuries, with cracked wheat, barley and other grains being the peasants' staples. Rice has since become a staple itself, in a variety of pilafs and many other dishes.

Some of the recipes call for medium grain rice, which is the equivalent in Greece of Italian *Arborio*. Most of the pilafs call for long-grain rice. I recommend Indian Basmati rice.

SAFFRON

Saffron is often sold powdered, but I prefer stigmas, which leave no opportunity for adulteration. The last time I bought saffron from an ordinary American shop it was $180 per oz, but don't despair. There are about 13,000 stigmas per ounce and it is usually packaged by the gram or less. It has always been so highly prized that Zeus is said to have slept on a bed of it. Put the stigmas in a cup with hot water and leave for 15-20 minutes, to infuse every golden drop of flavour and aroma.

SEMOLINA

Simygtháli is made of durum, the hardest type of wheat grown. It comes in three grades. The coarse and less coarse grades are used for milk puddings, halvas, some cakes and sweet breads, and this less coarse semolina is known as cream of wheat in the US. The fine grade is semolina flour, which is always yellow because it is unbleached. It is used worldwide for making pasta and is often sold as pasta or durum wheat flour. Don't be surprised by its texture, which is very fine but slightly coarser than ordinary hard flour because it is so much harder that it cannot be milled any smaller.

Greece and Sicily are unique in making this flour into great gorgeous loaves of country bread. If you can't find semolina or pasta flour for making bread, use ordinary unbleached strong flour instead.

THYME

There are many varieties of thyme in the world but the only one for me is *T. serpyllum*, which I call mountain thyme and which grows wild everywhere in Greece. Although oregano is more commonly associated with Greek cookery, you will find mountain thyme sprinkled more freely throughout these pages, because it grows in greater profusion on the island of Hydra where I live, and I have an unreasonable preference for it. If you buy dried Greek thyme or *thymári*, it is *Thymus serpyllum*: there is no other.

TOMATOES

It is difficult to imagine what Greek and Mediterranean cuisine must have been like before the end of the 16th century when the tomato was brought back from its native Peru by the Spanish. Those first tomatoes, little more than cherry-sized berries, were received with great scepticism. Today some varieties are comparative monsters. All the recipes in this book were originally made with luscious sun-ripened tomatoes. If your local varieties are uninspiringly anaemic, look for Italian plum tomatoes which are usually more flavourful. Failing that, use your own good judgement, adding extra tomato paste or sun-dried tomatoes, or turn to canned tomatoes which are an honorable product.

Domátes xerés, sun-dried tomatoes, are not used everywhere in Greece. They are a speciality of the island of Tinos – and the odd sensible individual with too many tomatoes. By soaking them in hot water and pulverizing them you can have home-made tomato paste. They add colour and tang to sauces, pastas, soups and stews. They are available in Italian delicatessens – also packed in oil, which is expensive but easy. And ironically the tasteless, under-ripe phenomena known as Californian tomatoes make wonderfully fresh, tart dried ones. You can replace 3-4 sun-dried tomatoes with 1 tablespoon tomato paste. However, I prefer to use sun-dried tomatoes unless the paste is home made.

The recipe I use for making my own paste was given to me by my friend Iris' grandmother. Purée 2.3 kg (5 lb) really ripe tomatoes in a food processor. This then goes into a non-aluminium pan with 2 tablespoons of salt, and a bay leaf, a sprig of thyme and a strip of lemon zest all tied in muslin. Cook this over low heat until most of the liquid has evaporated. Pour the paste in thin layers into large flat baking tins and leave in the sun to dry – covering them with muslin or a clean piece of screening to keep the critters out! Store in glass or earthenware jars, covered with a bay leaf and a layer of olive oil.

VINEGAR

The Spartans were infamous for their 'black broth', made of pork stock, salt and vinegar. And vinegar, *xýthi*, has been indispensable since the beginning of civilization in many a tastier dish. I have tried some vinegars in Greece so good that I wanted to drink them.

WILD GREENS

Wild greens, *hórta*, were domesticated by the neolithic revolution. But picking them wild has always been open to the poor, and this is still a ritual in Greece. The minute the scorching summer abates, the slightest bit of rain brings a profusion of edible weeds, until the next summer dries everything up again. *Hórta* is the general term for all wild green things and the kinds are endless – sometimes with different names in different places.

There are many wild greens with grandchildren or cousins at your green-grocer. *Róka* is rocket, known by its Italian name *arugula* in the US. It makes the best salad I know. *Vroúva* are mustard greens, whose domesticated cousins are eaten in the southern US states. *Vléeta,* wild beetroots, are the grandparents of cultivated ones, whose leaves can be eaten, and green chard. *Rathíkia* is the name for both dandelion and wild chicory, whose relatives are domesticated chicory, red radicchio and the curly endive. Don't throw away turnip tops or radish leaves. If they are very fresh, put them in the salad, or steam them or add to a soup or stew.

WINES AND SPIRITS

'Wine is the most beneficial of beverages, provided there is a happy combination of it with the occasion as well as with water,' said Plutarch. Like many good things in Greece, wine making is an institution, but not institutionalized. Many individuals still make their own wine, sometimes selling it locally. It is traditional for tavernas to make their own. Both resinated and unresinated wines are made – red, rosé and white, though I believe only the white retsina (resinated wine) is available internationally.

Since ancient times Greek wine has been fermented in vats smeared with pine resin as a preservative. It gives Greek wine its characteristic quality, though many outsiders find it a difficult taste to acquire.

The ancient word for wine was *oínos*. The modern word is *krasí*, the vessel in which wine (which was thick and sweet) was mixed with water before serving. So, literally it means a mixture.

Two commercial sweet wines, which may add an ancient flavour to the end of a meal, are Samos wine, from the muscat grape, and *mavrotháphne*, which is a rich, dark ruby port-like wine.

Metaxá brandy can be bought worldwide. Every family has its own recipe for cherry brandy, fig brandy, orange brandy and other secret infusions. Mine is to put a whole vanilla pod and three cardamon seeds, with two long strips of lemon zest into a bottle of *metaxá* and leave it to infuse for at least one month. Drink this straight, or use in baking.

Oúzo is distilled from the pulp which is left after the grapes have been crushed. It is flavoured with anise. *Rakí* and *tsípouro* are moonshine versions of *oúzo* and *gráppa* – fiery and smooth.

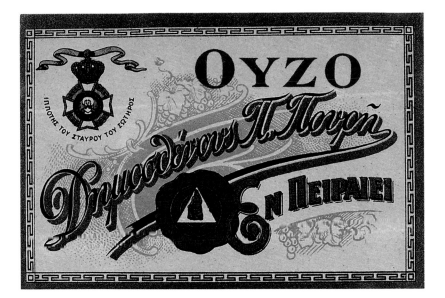

YOGURT

Yogurt, *yaoúrti*, must have been a staple in the Greek diet from ancient times, for the airborne bacteria, which cause the milk to sour, were as pervasive then as they are now. In the warm climate this is a necessary means of preserving milk. The delicious yogurt of Greece is made mostly from sheep's milk, often from cow's milk. Goat's milk is rather strong, unless mixed half and half with cow's milk.

Thick Greek yogurt, *yaoúrti tis sakoúlas*, is so thick and creamy that it can be used instead of *crème fraîche*. It is labelled 'strained', because it is hung up to drip in a cheese-cloth for a few hours, losing much of the liquid (and half its volume).

Although the commercial yogurt is superior, many Greeks still prefer to make it themselves. To make yogurt at home, use live yogurt for a starter. I don't believe commercial yogurt is the best for this purpose, though most brands will serve. Better, try to borrow a few spoonfuls – for example, from an Indian restaurant, as they are likely to make their own.

Heat 1 litre (1¾ pt) milk in a stainless steel or enamelled pan, bring to the boil, turn down and simmer for 1 minute. Remove from the heat and leave to cool until you can hold your finger in it for five seconds (the temperature should be 41-43°C/ 106-109°F if you have a cooking thermometer). Too hot, or too cold, milk causes failure.

In an earthenware or glass bowl, beat the starter with a few tablespoons of the hot milk until it is liquid. Slowly stir in the rest of the milk. Cover with a plate and wrap it in a blanket. Leave it undisturbed in a warm spot for about eight hours.

Refrigerate and use when chilled. Save a few spoonfuls to start your next batch. If you are using non-fat or low-fat milk, 2-3 tablespoons of dried milk solids dissolved in the hot milk will give it a thicker texture.

MEZÉTHES AND SOUPS

The little appetizers known as mezéthes are nibbled before, sometimes instead of, meals, while soups are indispensable to this rural cuisine.

From left to right VERÍKOKA YEMISTÁ (*p. 30*),
BOUREKÁKIA ME KREMITHÁKIA FRÉSKA (*p. 21*),
FÁVA ME LAHANIKÁ (*p. 25*),
PSAROSPANAKODOLMATHÁKIA (*p. 24*)

IMAGINE YOU ARE MEANDERING through the lanes and alleys of an island fishing village. The moon reflects on the whitewashed walls and the town glows in the dark. Windows and doors are open to let in the night air. As you pass along you hear heated discussions and snoring, laughter, televisions, of course, and music in the near distance ... *'Páme miá vólta sto fengári ...'* 'Let's go for a walk to the moon ...' is an old tune sung on countless nights like this, around countless tables in countless tavernas, gardens and cafés.

Across a clearing, under a couple of eucalyptus trees, is a table of singers and one rapt guitar player. They motion you to join them and pull up another chair. On the table there are jugs of Retsina and plates placed haphazardly to be shared among everyone. There are shiny, wrinkled olives, pungent pickled aubergines and salads of sun-ripened tomatoes, crisp cucumbers and onions. There are fried cheeses, smelts or pilchards, meatballs and grilled sausages – all with plenty of lemon wedges to squeeze over them. There is a plate of sliced lambs' tongues and a plate of sliced pink and white octopus, both in vinegar, oil and herbs. It is a simple feast of simple food to be enjoyed along with the night, the music and the company – an informal communion under the stars.

These *mezéthes*, or 'little bits', are a national Greek institution. They can be anything from a handful of olives offered in the middle of a field to a grand table spread lavishly as the prelude to a feast. Greek hospitality does not allow for anyone to enter a home without having just a 'little bit', whatever the time. Whether you call in the afternoon, or later in the evening when you may already have eaten dinner, you will be offered a little something. Nor would a Greek drink any sort of alcohol without some accompaniment and *oúzo* invariably means *mezéthes* to nibble alongside it, whether in the home, an *ouzerié* or taverna.

The word 'meze' is Turkish but the idea dates back at least as far as the 3rd century BC, when Lynceus characterized it '... for the cook sets before you a large plate on which are five small plates. One holds garlic, another a pair of sea urchins, another a sweet wine sop, another ten cockles, the last a small piece of sturgeon. While I am eating this, another is eating that; and while he is eating that, I have made away with this. What I want, good sir, is both the one and the other, but my wish is impossible. For I have neither five mouths nor five right hands ...' Poor Lynceus seems to have had the wrong idea, as it has never been in the Greek spirit to glut oneself.

In a tiny mountain village on Hydra, reached by a winding, rocky path, there used to live an old island curmudgeon. His granddaughter presides over the house now, but from a photograph he peers at you from behind a white moustache with the wingspan of an eagle. You can imagine him in the *salóni* barking orders for his meals. He wants soup before lunch, soup before dinner, soup, soup, soup.

Panaiotis was a rich old rascal with no rich continental pretensions about food, so he wanted the same hearty soup that probably comprised the entire meal next door at the shepherd's house. He liked *trahaná*, which is cracked wheat soaked in goat's milk and dried in the sun. It is then made into a porridge, with grated cheese over the top, or into a simple soup with the addition of water, onions, tomatoes and some wild herbs.

Another favourite is *patsás*, a hearty mixture of tripe, vegetables and pig's or lamb's trotters, always seasoned with *scorthostoúmbi*, garlic vinegar. In the 8th century BC, the poet Hesiod used to eat a viscous brew of mallows and during World War II the islanders ate so much nettle soup that they now prefer to forget its delicious bright greenness. *Mayerítsa* is the traditional Easter soup of lamb's innards and herbs thickened with *avgolémono*, egg and lemon sauce. There are also glorious fish soups and soups of chickpeas, beans, lentils, cracked wheat or barley. All are nourishing and pleasing. Wherever there has been a shell, a hollowed stone, an ox stomach or pot in which to cook it, there has been soup, timeless as the landscape that produces its ingredients.

BOUREKÁKIA ME KREMITHÁKIA FRÉSKA

SPRING ONIONS IN FILO

These cigarette-shaped *bourekákia* are light and elegant. They are quick to make and low in calories. The same method can be used for any filling – try chopped walnuts and Roquefort for a richer version, or fill them with leftovers for children's snacks.

If your filo pastry is frozen, as most commercial packets are, defrost it slowly in its package and then use immediately.

MAKES 16

*about 6 bunches spring onions,
white part and about 2.5 cm (1 in) green,
chopped, to make 350 g (12 oz)
125 ml (4 fl oz) olive oil
50 g (2 oz) fresh dill, chopped
salt and freshly ground black pepper
8 sheets filo pastry (see page 12), defrosted
2 tablespoons sesame seeds*

Toss the chopped onion in a bowl with 1 tablespoon olive oil, the chopped dill, salt and pepper.

Remove 8 sheets of filo from the package. Reseal the package and refrigerate it. Cover the filo you are using with a damp tea towel, well wrung out, and try to work hastily, as the pastry sheets have a tendency to dry out.

Lay out one sheet of filo and brush thoroughly with olive oil. Lay a second sheet over the first, and brush again with olive oil. Leaving a margin of 2.5 cm (1 in) down one short side of the filo, sprinkle a quarter of the onion mixture in a strip. Roll up from the same side, to make a long tube, packing the ends well. Place on a greased baking sheet.

Repeat this procedure three more times. Cut each tube diagonally into four sections, brush with olive oil and sprinkle the tops with sesame seeds. Bake in an oven preheated to 180°C (350°F, gas 4) until the tops are crisp and golden brown – about 30 minutes. They are good hot or cold.

KOLOKYTHÁKIA KEFTÉTHES

COURGETTE CROQUETTES

In Greece the islands have islands. One of ours looks, from Hydra, like a huge whale swimming through the sunset. It has one permanent inhabitant, two houses and one tiny shack of a taverna built to feed the archaeological diving crew working there in the summer and the occasional yacht. From time to time we have a boatman ferry us over, and there we watch the moon come up while we nibble these croquettes and wait for a baby kid to come off the spit.

In Greece anything that has been deep-fried is invariably drained on newspaper, rather than on kitchen paper!

MAKES 24

*100 g (4 oz) courgettes, grated
25 g (1 oz) leek, grated
65 g (2½ oz) kefalotýri cheese, or Italian sardo
or Parmesan, grated
50 g (2 oz) finely ground paximáthia (see page 10)
or toasted breadcrumbs
3 tablespoons finely chopped flat leaf parsley
2 tablespoons finely chopped fresh mint leaves
2 medium-sized eggs
salt and freshly ground black pepper
about 450 ml (¾ pt) olive oil for frying*

Layer the grated courgettes in a sieve, salting well, and leave to drain for 20 minutes. Rinse and squeeze out any excess liquid. Combine all the ingredients in a bowl, stirring until they are evenly mixed.

Heat oil to come about 2 cm (¾ in) deep in a wok, or wide pan with reasonably high sides, until the surface begins to tremble and the oil splutters loudly when sprinkled with 1-2 drops of water (stand well back as you try this). Push heaped teaspoons of the mixture into the oil, and fry until a bronze colour (a couple of minutes), turning them over once. Please don't crowd the pan or the temperature will drop, causing the croquettes to absorb the oil and become greasy. Drain on kitchen paper and serve piping hot.

TYROPITÁKIA TIS KIRÍAS SOPHÍAS

KIRIA SOPHIA'S CHEESE FRITTERS

Half an hour's walk from home, in the shadow of a rocky ridge that was an ancient Mycenaean lookout, there is a fishing village where Kiria Sophia taught me to make these little cheese fritters. She says everyone makes them, but I have yet to come across any quite like these.

They are easy, fast and delicious with any combination of cheeses, something you can make, at a pinch, when you have little bits and pieces of cheese left in the refrigerator. Try them with the addition of fresh herbs or caraway seeds.

MAKES ABOUT 48

160 g (5½ oz) féta cheese, crumbled
160 g (5½ oz) kefalograviéra cheese,
or Gruyère or Emmental, diced
160 g (5½ oz) kasséri cheese, or cheddar, diced
50 g (2 oz) plain flour
50 ml (2 fl oz) milk
1-2 medium-sized eggs
olive oil for deep frying

Put all three cheeses in a bowl and sprinkle with the flour. Moisten them with the milk, adding a tablespoon at a time, so the mixture feels silky. Beat in the eggs one at a time, as you might not need both. If a cohesive goo forms with one egg, omit the other.

Heat the oil in a deep-fat fryer, wok or a wide pan with reasonably high sides, until the surface trembles. The oil will make a high pitched sound or crackle when sprinkled with 1-2 drops of water (stand well back if you try this). Push heaped teaspoonfuls of the mixture into the hot oil, being careful not to crowd the pan. (If the pan is overcrowded, the temperature of the oil will drop, and the fritters will then absorb the oil, making them greasy.)

Fry the fritters for 1 minute, turning them once. When they are the colour of old varnish, remove them onto kitchen paper to drain and fry the next batch. Serve them piping hot.

ELIÉS STO FOÚRNO

BAKED OLIVES

If you don't want to wait for wonderful, marinated olives that appear from the recesses of well-organized larders, these baked olives should delight you, hot or cold. Originally the dish of olives would have been placed by the side of a fire to heat and macerate.

MAKES 500 G (1 LB)

500 g (1 lb) Greek olives, any variety;
they can even be mixed
450 ml (16 fl oz) red wine
4 garlic cloves, sliced
2 bay leaves
4 strips of thinly pared lemon zest,
each about 5 cm (2 in) long
1 teaspoon dried mountain thyme (see page 16)
40 ml (1½ fl oz) mastíha liquor (see page 14)
or oúzo
6 twists of the pepper mill

Combine all the ingredients in a flameproof casserole and bake, covered, in an oven preheated to 180°C (350°F, gas 4) for 30 minutes.

BÁMIES XEROTIGANISMÉNES

CRISP FRIED OKRA

I say this dish serves 8-10 people, but that is only the case if your guests do not become immediately addicted to them. These little crunchies have become the downfall of many of my friends.

SERVES 8-10

1 kg (2 lb) okra
700 ml (1 pt 4 fl oz) olive oil for frying
salt and cayenne pepper

To clean okra (ladies' fingers), wipe off the bristle with a towel. Cut away the stem without opening the pod, and soak in 125 ml (4 fl oz) vinegar, with a little salt, in a shallow dish. This is best left in the sun for 2 hours. Rinse the okra well and drain. This has the effect of removing the sticky juice, which would make these fritters soft.

Dry them well and slice the okra into 1 cm (½ in) pieces. Heat the oil in a wok, deep-fat fryer or a wide pan with reasonably high sides, until the surface starts to tremble. The oil should crackle if you sprinkle it with a few drops of water (stand well back).

OUTSIDE A KAFENEION As soon as the warmer days arrive, chairs and tables are moved outdoors and much of life goes on in the open.

Fry the okra by scattering it into the oil, about a cup at a time, so that the temperature of the oil does not drop too far. Stir it with a slotted spoon to turn the pieces in the oil. When the okra is burnished brown – 1–2 minutes – it will be crisp. Remove with the slotted spoon and drain on kitchen paper. Sprinkle with salt and cayenne and serve.

PSAROSPANAKODOLMATHÁKIA

SPINACH PARCELS WITH FISH PILAF

This dish was inspired by time, place and leftovers. The time is the eve of the twenty-first century when many dishes are being rediscovered, resynthesized and reinvented. The place is the Greek islands, where the simplicity of life in a sparse landscape mixes gracefully with a little oriental refinement. The leftovers were those from the grouper with vegetables (the recipe for which is on page 96). The result is an old dish in a new package which has probably been reinvented many times before on these same Greek islands.

Steamed fish, canned salmon or luxurious smoked salmon are all good in these parcels. Serve them hot with egg and lemon sauce (*see page 104*) as a first course for six or lunch for four, or plain and cold as an excellent hors d'oeuvre. If you cook the dish in the early months of the year, use the juice of Seville (bitter) oranges, and substitute orange juice for lemon in the egg and lemon sauce.

MAKES ABOUT 24

*24 or more large, unblemished spinach leaves,
washed and thick stalks removed*
*1 medium-sized leek, cleaned and
white finely chopped*
4 tablespoons fruity olive oil
100 g (4 oz) long-grain rice
*250 g (8 oz) leftover cooked fish, or drained
canned (or smoked) salmon*
*100 g (4 oz) mizíthra cheese, or ricotta
or cottage cheese*
25 g (1 oz) flat leaf parsley, finely chopped
25 g (1 oz) fresh dill, finely chopped
*25 g (1 oz) spring onion, white and light green,
finely chopped*
salt and freshly ground black pepper
*2 Seville (bitter) oranges, or 1 lemon
and 1 sweet orange*

Drop the spinach leaves into boiling water, a few at a time, and blanch for about 1 minute – just long enough to make them pliable for rolling. Remove them with a slotted spoon or chopsticks and transfer to cold water. Drain them, then lay them out flat.

In a heavy frying-pan fry the chopped leek in 3 tablespoons olive oil, over low heat, until it becomes transparent. Sprinkle in the rice and sauté until it, too, becomes transparent. Stir in between 125-175 ml (4-6 fl oz) water, adding about 50 ml (2 fl oz) at a time. Let this become absorbed, before you pour in more. When the rice is almost – but not quite – done remove it from the heat. Toss the rice with the fish, cheese, herbs and spring onion and season.

Lay out one spinach leaf flat and place a spoonful of the rice mixture at the widest part of the leaf. Loosely roll it up, folding the sides over the middle after the first turn. You should have made a neat little packet, with just enough extra room for the rice to expand a little. Repeat until all the filling is used.

Lay extra blanched spinach leaves in the bottom of a ceramic or ovenproof baking dish, with a few thinly-pared strips of orange (and lemon) zest. Pack in your *dolmathákia* in a single layer, so they are touching one another. Drizzle them with the remaining tablespoon of olive oil. Squeeze the juice of the oranges (and lemon if using) and heat through. Pour this over the *dolmathákia*. If the juice does not come nearly to the top, then make up the difference with hot water.

Cover the dish tightly and cook in an oven preheated to 180°C (350°F, gas 4) for about 25-30 minutes. Serve hot with egg and lemon sauce (*see page 104*), or cold without it.

FÁVA ME LAHANIKÁ

YELLOW SPLIT-PEA DIP
WITH RAW VEGETABLES

In a simple island taverna it is not uncommon to find *fáva*, *keftéthes*, meatballs, *féta* and tomatoes the only things to eat. I know a traditionalist who claims that this *fáva* is not really *fáva* because its essence has been changed from something humble to something else. Normally the split-pea purée is simply plopped onto a plate, then oil is poured over it, with lemon and onions cut into little boats to use as scoops. I like it both as its essential and unessential self.

SERVES 6-8

*175 g (6 oz) yellow split peas, soaked overnight
in cold water
pinch of bicarbonate of soda
125 g (4½ oz) onion, roughly chopped
5 garlic cloves, peeled, 1 clove very finely chopped
or puréed
salt
finely grated zest and juice of 1 large lemon
125-175 ml (4-6 fl oz) fruity olive oil*

TO SERVE

*assorted raw vegetables, such as courgettes,
carrots, celery, turnips and onions, cut into sticks*

Drain the soaked split peas and put into a saucepan with fresh cold water. Add the bicarbonate of soda – no more than ¹⁄₁₆th of a teaspoon – and bring to the boil. Drain and rinse them. Cover again with cold water and bring to the boil.

Add the onion and 4 whole cloves of garlic. Cover and simmer for about 1½ hours, until the peas turn to complete mush. Keep checking to see that the water does not boil away, but be careful not to drown them. Towards the end help them along by mashing.

When the peas are done, remove from the heat, salt well and leave until cold. Then mash and beat to a purée, adding in the puréed or very finely chopped garlic clove, and the grated zest and juice of the lemon. Add the oil, a little at a time, stopping when the purée seems to have absorbed enough. Taste and season. Serve surrounded by vegetables for dipping.

SCORTHOSTOÚMBI

PICKLED GARLIC AND GARLIC
VINEGAR

Pickled garlic is a wonderful snack, hors d'oeuvre or garnish. Try it in a martini instead of the classic olive. The vinegar from this pickle, too, is divine in a salad, or used as a condiment. There isn't a longshoreman in any port in Greece who doesn't anoint his *fasolátha*, bean soup, or *patsás*, tripe soup, with *scorthostoúmbi* in the dark and weary early morning hours.

I found the pickled garlic especially handy in Greece when the garlic supply used to disappear in the winter months. Now, of course, garlic is imported into Greece from as far away as Argentina, when it is out of season.

I make this with fresh, spring garlic, which I don't believe is commercially available elsewhere. Please use the freshest garlic available – it should be crunchy and unblemished.

MAKES 1 LITRE (2 PT) JAR

*6 good heads of garlic, about 200 g (7 oz), peeled
4 sprigs fresh thyme
1 teaspoon peppercorns
2 strips lemon zest, about 5 cm (2 in) long
¼ teaspoon citric acid
700 ml (1 pt 4 fl oz) good wine vinegar
1 small, hot fresh chilli, whole*

Sterilize a 1 litre (2 pt) glass jar with boiling water. Layer the garlic cloves in it with the thyme, peppercorns and strips of lemon zest.

Dissolve the citric acid in the vinegar and pour it over the layered garlic. Add the chilli to the top, cover and store in a dark cupboard, or the refrigerator, for two weeks before opening.

IDYLLIC PASTURES *(overleaf) A lone goat enjoys the lush grass in a sunlit olive grove.*

ANGINÁRES TARAMÁ

COLD ARTICHOKES WITH TARAMA MAYONNAISE

My friend Pheni had an old aunt, nicknamed 'Madame la marquise', who always greeted her by saying, 'You may kiss me but I have no time to speak to you now'. When 'Madame la marquise' finally spoke to her niece, she found that Pheni was already a grown woman, charming and larger than life in every way. To make up for lost time, the 'marquise' gave Pheni this recipe.

The *taramosaláta* can be served by itself, with bread or raw vegetables. If you serve it on its own, though, triple the recipe, or it will be inhaled in seconds. It looks very nice served in the cup of artichoke leaves, but I rarely do this myself, because I love those tender inner leaves.

This version of *taramosaláta* is much lighter than most, as it has no bread in it. This means it is also more prone to curdle. If it does, the 'marquise' advises adding a small mashed, boiled potato and continuing as if nothing ever happened.

SERVES 6

6 small fresh artichokes
2 large juicy lemons, about 250 g (8 oz) altogether
salt and freshly ground white pepper
40 g (1½ oz) taramá (see page 12),
rinsed if necessary, or
50g (2 oz) smoked skinned cod's roe
1 tablespoon finely grated onion pulp
250 ml (8 fl oz) fruity olive oil

To clean the artichokes, cut off the stems flush with the bottom, remove any tough, unsightly outer leaves and cut off the top one-third of the flower bud itself. Force the leaves open a little, and rinse under cold running water. Keep the artichokes in a large bowl of water, with a squeeze of lemon or a splash of vinegar to prevent discolouring.

Place the artichokes upside down in a pot large enough to hold them all in one layer and pour in

ORNAMENTAL BASIL *This herb is found on many island windowsills, loved for its decorative qualities.*

boiling water to come one-quarter of the way up their sides. Salt and simmer 15-40 minutes, depending on their age and size – until the heart is just tender when pricked with a fork. Drain and refresh them under cold water; drain again and chill.

Beat the *taramá* or smoked cod's roe with the grated onion. You can do this easily in a food processor. Finely grate the zest of one lemon and beat in, with 2 teaspoons boiling water.

Squeeze the juice of both lemons. Alternately dribble in lemon juice and olive oil, beating each addition in before adding the next, as though making mayonnaise – it may not need all the oil. If you are doing this by hand, it takes perseverance and elbow grease to make it nice and light. Taste and season with pepper. Open the artichokes and remove the inner, soft leaves and then the hairy choke. Spoon *taramá* into the cup of leaves.

SALINGÁRIA

SNAILS IN TOMATO SAUCE

During the dry months of July, August and September, when the wild greens have withered, you will still see the occasional human in the Greek countryside, caringly bent – this time collecting dormant snails. In fact, this is a good way to keep your own garden snail-free, as long as you don't use harmful pesticides that may come back at you – and you clean the snails properly *(see note)*.

Open crates of sleeping snails collected in the mountains of Crete are available at our local *bakáliko*, grocer. If you are not inclined to collect your own, you can use canned snails very successfully for this recipe.

Greeks can eat plates full of these snails and 10-12 per person would never be enough, especially as Greek snails are much smaller than the huge French varieties seen elsewhere. If you learn to love these, as the Greeks do, then increase the amounts accordingly. By adding 140 g (4½ oz) rice and 250 ml (8 fl oz) water, this becomes a main-course pilaf.

SERVES 4-6

50-60 dormant snails: these have white, dried
mucous sealing the opening,
or 200 g (7 oz) canned snails

TOMATO SAUCE

1 large onion, 250 g (8 oz), finely chopped
3-4 tablespoons olive oil
600 g (1 lb 6 oz) tomatoes, skinned, seeded and
flesh finely chopped
2 garlic cloves, finely chopped
¼ teaspoon freshly ground cinnamon
½ teaspoon freshly ground black pepper
salt
1 bay leaf, crumbled
15 g (½ oz) fresh mint leaves, finely chopped
50 ml (2 fl oz) oúzo, or
other anise-flavoured liquor

Put dormant snails into a large pot, with a heavy top, and moisten with water. Use enough water to waken the sleeping snails – about 250 ml (8 fl oz) – but not too much to drown them. Cover and weight the lid well, to prevent finding snails crawling all over your kitchen (a few volumes of the Encyclopedia Britannica do very well). You will hear them gurgling, crawling up the sides of the pot and falling back in, when they are revived. Rinse them and repeat.

This time, when they have re-emerged from their shells, weight the lid of the pot and put them over a very slow flame. As the water slowly reaches boiling point, they will die unaware, without retreating into their shells, where they are then difficult to reach. Steam them for 10 minutes, adding a little more water if necessary.

While the snails are steaming, fry the onion in the olive oil over low heat until transparent. Add the tomatoes, garlic, cinnamon, pepper, salt, bay leaf, mint and *oúzo*, cover and simmer for 10 minutes.

Drain the cooked snails and rinse them with cold water. By inserting the point of a small, sharp paring knife into the seam of the spiral of the shell, pop off part of the conical end of the shell. Scrape out the little black bit (which is called the *cloaca*, and is the snail's stomach), if you see it.

Put the cleaned snails into the sauce. Canned snails can be added here, with the shells that are sold with them. Simmer for 40 minutes, until tender. Eating fresh snails is not a delicate matter. Pick them up with your fingers and suck out the flesh. Some of them may need some coaxing with a toothpick. Mop up the sauce with crusty bread and enjoy it!

Note: Dormant snails conveniently purge their own insides and in cold countries snails can be collected after hibernation in late winter. But if they are live and crawling when you collect them, you will have to purge them and it is dangerous to skip this, as they may have eaten something that is poisonous for you.

The simplest method is to put them in a covered bucket in a cool dry place and starve them until a calcareous membrane forms across the mouth – about 2 weeks. You can then treat them like dormant ones.

BISCÓTA-KÍMINO

CUMIN BISCUITS

When she heard I was writing this book, my friend Martha, from Texas, asked me to include this little recipe within a recipe:

A little oúzo in the moussaka
A little oúzo in the cook
Serve on terrace with 360 degrees
Of panoramic view

. . . which is exactly what I do with these biscuits. They are divine at sunset dunked into a glass of *oúzo*.

MAKES ABOUT 36

500 g (18 oz) plain flour, plus extra for shaping
125 g (4 oz) caster sugar
½ teaspoon salt
finely grated zest of 2 medium-sized lemons
2 medium-sized eggs, beaten
50-100 ml (2-3½ fl oz) oúzo or other anise-flavoured liquor
3 tablespoons cumin seeds, lightly toasted then roughly crushed with pestle and mortar
1½ teaspoons baking powder

Combine the flour, sugar, salt and grated lemon zest in a mixing bowl. Whisk the eggs with the smaller quantity of *oúzo* (you can use more later if the dough seems dry). Beat this into the dry ingredients until well absorbed. Add the baking powder to the crushed cumin seeds and then mix this thoroughly into the dough.

On a well-floured surface make half the dough into a sausage shape, about 45 cm (18 in) long. If it holds its shape too well, it probably has too much flour, and you should work in a little more *oúzo*. Transfer the shaped loaf to an oiled, or non-stick, baking sheet, and repeat with the other half of the dough. Place the two loaves far enough apart to allow for spreading – which they should already have started doing.

Bake the loaves in an oven preheated to 180°C (350°F, gas 4), for 45-50 minutes. Remove them, cool for 10 minutes, and then cut into 2.5 cm (1 in) slices.

Arrange these in one layer on the baking sheet and return them to the oven to dry out – about 10 minutes, turning them over half way through. If you let them dry out too much, they will become jaw breakers, while if you don't let them dry out thoroughly, they won't keep well. Like everything in life, they should be just right. Cool and store in an airtight container.

VERÍKOKA YEMISTÁ

APRICOTS FILLED WITH SMOKED TROUT

The Egyptians credited the Greeks with inventing smoking as a means of preserving food and the Greeks do it extremely well to this day. When choosing smoked trout, it should be firm – not mushy – and should not smell too strongly of smoke. Island-ripened, sun-ripened apricots are a poem. If you can find a poetic apricot, or one that isn't too hard to ripen or too mushy and tasteless, then these canapés taste like spring itself.

They can also be made with smoked eel, or peach or nectarine halves.

MAKES 24

12 luscious apricots
1 smoked trout, about 250 g (8 oz), skinned, filleted and flaked
½ cucumber, about 250 g (8 oz), peeled, seeds removed and flesh diced
1 fat spring onion (about 2 teaspoons), finely chopped
1 tablespoon finely chopped fresh dill
1 teaspoon fresh lemon juice
1 tablespoon fruity olive oil
salt and freshly ground black pepper

Wash the apricots and halve them through the seam. Remove the stones. In a mixing bowl carefully toss together the flaked trout, cucumber dice, chopped onion, dill, lemon juice and olive oil, and season. Pile a spoonful of the salad on each apricot half and arrange prettily on a platter.

KATSIKÁKI PATÉ

LAMB OR KID TERRINE

You can buy a whole or half baby kid from an island butcher here. There are few precise cuts with names, which happily forces one to develop ways of using the trimmings. Talk to your butcher about using inexpensive cuts of lamb, or his trimmings, for this terrine which should be made ahead and eaten after a few days. It is ideal for a sunny spring lunch, particularly a picnic, with tomato soup, olives, capers, pickles and lots of country bread.

You can make a nice lunch for two from the lamb shanks which are left. These can be served cold or hot, with boiled vegetables and a little broth or jellied consommé.

SERVES 8

500 g (1 lb) young lamb or kid meat, fat, gristle and
tendons removed, cut into cubes
½ teaspoon fresh thyme leaves, or ¼ teaspoon dried
mountain thyme (see page 16)
4 tablespoons cognac
2 medium-sized eggs
350 ml (12 fl oz) thick yogurt, sour cream or
crème fraîche
1 tablespoon olive oil
1 teaspoon salt
½ teaspoon ground white pepper
50 g (2 oz) pine nuts
4 bay leaves

JELLY

2 lamb (or kid) shanks
1 veal knuckle, cracked
1 medium-sized onion, stuck with 1 clove
1 carrot
1 handful parsley stalks (why waste them?)
1 handful celery tops and leaves
2 bay leaves
10 black peppercorns
salt

Make the pelté, or jelly, for this dish a day ahead, as chilling and skimming is the best way. Put the lamb (or kid) shanks and the veal bone in a pot and add about 1 litre (2 pt) cold water to cover. Bring to the boil, uncovered (to keep the broth from becoming cloudy). Skim, then add the remaining ingredients. Simmer for 2-3 hours until reduced by almost half. This should make a nice jelly. Strain through a dampened cheesecloth or muslin, and chill.

Meanwhile, marinate the cubed meat with the thyme and cognac for four hours at room temperature (or overnight in the refrigerator).

Work the meat in a food processor until it is as smooth as you can get it, or mince finely. (The old tried-and-true method is to pound the meat in a mortar with a pestle and then force through a sieve.) Beat in the eggs, one at a time, then the yogurt, sour cream or crème fraîche and finally the olive oil, salt and pepper.

Scrape the mixture into a bowl and stir in the pine nuts, trying to incorporate them evenly.

Oil the sides and bottom of an 850 ml (1½ pt) earthenware or ovenproof glass baking dish. Press the meat mixture into this and arrange the bay leaves on top in a pattern. Cover with foil.

Stand the dish in a baking tin and pour in boiling water to come halfway up the side.

Cook the terrine in an oven preheated to 180°C (350°F, gas 4) for 1¼-1½ hours. When the juices that rise to the surface are clear, the terrine is done. Remove from the oven and weight with something that fits inside the rim of the dish. When it is cold, refrigerate it.

The next day scrape the fat from the top and pour in the melted jelly to cover it well. Chill again. The terrine is at its best after three or four days.

FASOLÁTHA

WHITE BEAN SOUP

This must be the most frequently eaten and favourite winter soup in all of Greece. But even this simple bean soup has many points of debate. Carrots or no carrots? Tomatoes or no tomatoes? Garlic or no garlic? If your tap water is hard, use bottled water to soak and cook the beans, otherwise they will never soften.

SERVES 6-8

400 g (14 oz) medium-sized white beans like
cannellini, soaked overnight in cold water
500 g (1 lb) onions, thinly sliced
3 tablespoons fruity olive oil
½ teaspoon sugar
250 g (8 oz) carrots, sliced or diced
tops and leaves of 6 celery stalks, chopped
3 garlic cloves, sliced
4 tablespoons finely chopped fresh savory
1 bay leaf
1 clove
1 small hot fresh red chilli, whole, or ¼-½ teaspoon
cayenne pepper, to taste
salt

Drain the beans, cover them with fresh water and boil for 10 minutes. Drain them and just cover again with hot water. Bring them back to the boil, cover and simmer for about 1-1½ hours, until tender.

While the beans are simmering, sauté the onions in the olive oil until they turn red-brown, adding splashes of water to keep them from burning. Sprinkle the onions with sugar, and cook for a minute to caramelize, stirring occasionally. Add the carrots, celery, sliced garlic, savory, bay leaf, clove and chilli or cayenne. Sauté for 2-3 minutes.

When the beans are tender add the sautéed vegetables and 2.4 litres (4 pt) water and bring back to the boil. Simmer for 15 minutes, until the beans are very soft. Add salt to taste and serve with crusty bread or the *kouloúria* – sesame seed rings – on page 49.

FASOLÁTHA *left*, KOULOÚRIA *right (p. 49)*

FAKI ME SPANÁKI

LENTIL SOUP WITH SPINACH

Lentil soup is traditionally served with a bottle of vinegar, *scorthostoúmbi*, on the table, to splash into your bowl. I like to sprinkle a little fresh basil over my soup as well. And I usually have olives and capers on the table to toss in at will.

SERVES 6-8

350 g (12 oz) large green or brown dried lentils,
soaked for 2 hours in cold water
250 g (8 oz) onions, chopped
1 medium-sized leek, cleaned and chopped
3 tablespoons olive oil
250 g (8 oz) carrots, diced
300 g (10 oz) waxy potatoes, washed and diced
6-7 garlic cloves (40g [1½ oz]), sliced
100 g (4 oz) flat leaf parsley, finely chopped
2 bay leaves
1 clove
1 tablespoon mountain thyme (see page 16)
1 teaspoon oregano (see page 15)
1 teaspoon freshly ground black pepper
salt
1 kg (2 lb) spinach, thick stalks removed and washed
40 g (1½ oz) fresh basil leaves, chopped

In a large pot, about 7 litres (12 pt) capacity, fry the chopped onions and leek in the olive oil over low heat until transparent. Add the carrots, potatoes, garlic, parsley, bay leaves, clove, thyme and oregano, and sprinkle with pepper. Stir over a medium-high heat for a few minutes.

Drain and rinse the lentils. Stir them into the vegetables and add 3 litres (5 pt) water. Simmer until the lentils are soft – about 40-45 minutes. Please don't add salt until the end, or the lentils will take much longer to cook. In fact, they may never soften.

Add the salt, chop the spinach and stir it in, with half the chopped basil. Serve as soon as the spinach has wilted. The extra basil is for sprinkling on top at table.

TAHINÓSOUPA

SESAME PASTE SOUP WITH SAFFRON AND GARLIC

This is a classic example of the ingenuity exercised in the kitchen during Lent, resulting in a simple, elegant and nourishing dish. I like to leave the saffron threads intact, floating in an ochre sea of soup. If you want to make it even more beautiful, float an edible nasturtium in each bowl.

SERVES 6

1.5 litres (2 pt 8 fl oz) herb broth (see page 37)
or water
salt and freshly ground black pepper
75 g (3 oz) long-grain rice
30 strands saffron, soaked in 50 ml (2 fl oz)
boiling water
250 g (8 oz) light tahini (sesame seed paste)
finely grated zest of 1 lemon, plus 1 tablespoon
of juice
2 garlic cloves, finely chopped
15 g (½ oz) flat leaf parsley, finely chopped

Bring the herb broth or water to the boil, salt it and add the rice. Cook for 15 minutes. When it is nearly done, add the saffron with its liquid.

In the meantime, beat the tahini, with 125 ml (4 fl oz) cold water, the finely grated zest from the lemon, 1 tablespoon lemon juice and the garlic.

When the rice is cooked, slowly pour 2 ladlefuls of saffron broth into the tahini, and then pour it back into the pot. Stir well and serve each bowl garnished with a sprinkling of chopped parsley.

SOÚPA-MANITÁRIA

WILD MUSHROOM SOUP

Imagine you are in a shepherd's hut at the remotest end of a remote Greek island. There are herbs growing in pots on the windowsill and a small vegetable patch outside. The rafters are lined with ripening cheeses and hung with bags of barley, rice and wheat. Strings of dried garlic, onions and tomatoes adorn the whitewashed walls. There is a pail of goat's milk in the corner. Outside the sheep and goats graze on the same plants the shepherd picks for salads or for steaming, and the pine forest is pervaded by the musty smell of mushrooms. The scene is set for this soup.

SERVES 4-5

700 g (1½ lb) fresh wild mushrooms such as chanterelles, or the same weight of cultivated mushrooms with 40 g (1½ oz) dried wild mushrooms, such as ceps

salt

6 sun-dried tomatoes, pounded (see page 16) or 1½ tablespoons tomato paste

100 g (4 oz) onion, thinly sliced

50 ml (2 fl oz) fruity olive oil

2 garlic cloves, finely chopped

50 g (2 oz) flat leaf parsley or celery tops and leaves, chopped

1.5 litres (2 pt 8 fl oz) herb broth (see page 37) or other stock

25 g (1 oz) barley flakes or pearl barley

250 ml (8 fl oz) goat's milk, herb broth or water

freshly ground black pepper

If using dried mushrooms, soak them in hot water with ½ teaspoon salt added, for 30 minutes. Drain the liquid through a sieve lined with a damp muslin and reserve. Rinse the soaked mushrooms under water to remove any grit, and chop them roughly.

Sprinkle the fresh mushrooms with salt and let them sit for a few minutes, then wipe them with a damp cloth. In Greece the mushrooms are often very dirty, and we need to soak them in a little salted water

BEAST OF BURDEN *Donkeys are essential as carriers of farm produce and goods on the islands*

for a few minutes to loosen the dirt before we wipe and slice them.

Cut dry tomatoes into little pieces with the kitchen scissors and soak them in 125 ml (4 fl oz) boiling broth (or stock) for 30 minutes. Drain the liquid into the reserved mushroom liquid. Crush the pulp of soaked tomatoes to a rough paste with pestle and mortar.

In a heavy-bottomed pot, fry the onion in the olive oil over low heat until transparent. Add the mushrooms – both fresh and dried – and garlic and stir for 2 minutes. Add the tomato paste, parsley or celery and reserved juices, and stir another 2 minutes. Pour in the herb broth and the barley, and simmer about 30 minutes. Stir in the goat's milk and stir over low heat for 2-3 minutes, without boiling. Taste and season with pepper and salt if needed. Serve with crusty bread and a green salad.

DOMATÓSOUPA

TOMATO SOUP

If you go to Angeliki, a spritely *yiayiá* (grandmother), with an ailment, she commiserates and sends you away. Next day she tells you she dreamed that you should go up the mountain, pick this and that, make an infusion and drink it every day for a week. Her cures sometimes work, never hurt and always taste good, like the herb broth in this recipe.

SERVES 4-6

1 large mild Spanish onion, finely chopped
1 medium-sized leek, washed and finely chopped
3 tablespoons fruity olive oil
600 g (1¼ lb) tomatoes, skinned, seeded and finely chopped
3 sun-dried tomatoes, snipped up and soaked in 125 ml (4 fl oz) boiling water, or 2 teaspoons tomato paste
1 teaspoon sugar
1 garlic clove, finely chopped
finely grated zest of ½ orange
2 tablespoons finely chopped fresh mint
350 ml (12 fl oz) thick yogurt or sour cream
1 heaped tablespoon flour
salt and freshly ground pepper
25 g (1 oz) flat leaf parsley, finely chopped

HERB BROTH

2 tablespoons fresh chopped thyme or 1 tablespoon dried
2 bay leaves
2 tablespoons fresh marjoram or 1 tablespoon dried oregano
1 sprig of fresh parsley
2 strips of lemon zest, about 5 cm (2 in) long
100 g (4 oz) onion
4 garlic cloves
1 small, hot dried red chilli, whole, or ½ teaspoon cayenne pepper
10 black peppercorns
1 clove
1 small piece of cinnamon bark
salt

For those who want a quick and easy soup base, throw all the broth ingredients into a saucepan with 1.2 litres (2 pt) water and bring to the boil. Simmer for 10-15 minutes, strain and use.

To make the soup, use a heavy-bottomed soup pot to fry the onion and leek in the olive oil over low heat until transparent. Add the chopped tomato flesh. Pound the sun-dried tomatoes with their liquid to a paste with pestle and mortar (it does not have to be completely smooth), then add to the pot with the sugar (or use the tomato paste). Continue cooking on a fairly high heat for 2-3 minutes. Add the garlic, grated orange zest and mint, and cook, stirring, for another 2-3 minutes. Slowly add the herb broth, cover and simmer for 30-45 minutes. (You can make the soup ahead to this point.)

In a bowl, beat the yogurt (or cream) and flour until smooth. In a steady stream, slowly pour in a ladleful of hot soup, while continuing to beat. Repeat with one more ladleful and then slowly pour this back into the soup, stirring constantly. Continue stirring over very low heat for 7-10 minutes. Do not boil, or you might have a curdled mess.

Taste and season, then add the fresh parsley. Serve immediately with crusty country bread. A green salad, olives and a slice of *féta* cheese go well with it.

DOMATÓSOUPA *above,* KOLOKYTHÓSOUPA *below (p. 38)*

KOLOKYTHÓSOUPA

PUMPKIN SOUP

My neighbour came to me recently and asked for a pumpkin soup recipe. I was delighted to give her this one, but mystified when she returned later with a potful of tasteless slop. Before I tore up the recipe, I asked her how she had made it. She used four kilos of pumpkin instead of one. She had no onion and only a small leek. It looked too thin so she drained off most of the stock. And she used old spices that smelled like the inside of a musty dungeon. Please, please, please remember that pre-ground spices, even at their freshest, are not as deliciously pungent as freshly ground. Increase the amounts for pre-ground and please throw them out if they have no aroma.

The colours of pale pumpkin, purple onion and green parsley are something beautiful to behold in this soup.

SERVES 6

1 kg pumpkin (2 lb), cubed
300 g (10 oz) mild Spanish onion, sliced
1 large leek, white and tender part of green sliced to make 200 g (7 oz)
3 tablespoons fruity olive oil
salt and ground white pepper
½ teaspoon freshly ground coriander seed
1/16 teaspoon freshly ground cinnamon
1/16 teaspoon freshly ground allspice
1/16 teaspoon freshly ground clove
2 tablespoons oúzo, or other anise-flavoured liquor
900 ml (1 pt 12 fl oz) stock or water
250 ml (8 fl oz) thick cream or yogurt
1 tablespoon semolina (optional)

GARNISH

150 g (5 oz) purple onion, thinly sliced
2 tablespoons olive oil
50 g (2 oz) flat leaf parsley, chopped

In a heavy soup pot, fry the onion and leek in the olive oil over low heat until transparent. Add the pumpkin and continue frying for 3-5 minutes. Sprinkle with the salt, pepper and spices and fry for a further 1-2 minutes. Add the oúzo and a little water, to ensure the vegetables do not burn. Lower the heat and braise until the pumpkin is tender, 30-40 minutes.

Remove the pot from the heat and purée the vegetables in a food processor, or through a vegetable mill. Return the purée to the pot and thin it with stock or water. Heat the soup through, add the cream or yogurt and stir until just hot again. If the soup is too thin for your taste, sprinkle in the semolina and simmer for another 5-10 minutes, until the soup has thickened and the semolina is cooked. If you do this, be careful not to let it boil or the yogurt will separate. Season well.

Meanwhile fry the sliced purple onion in olive oil over low heat until transparent, and stir this into the soup at the end, with the parsley.

SOÚPA TSATZÍKI

COLD YOGURT SOUP

Anyone who has ever been to a Greek taverna has surely eaten *tsatzíki*, a thick, garlicky yogurt dip. Here is a refreshingly cool summer soup made from that old standby.

SERVES 4

½ cucumber, peeled, seeded and flesh grated
salt to taste
500 ml (18 fl oz) thick yogurt
1 garlic clove, very finely chopped
finely grated rind and juice of 1 lemon (optional)
2 tablespoons finely chopped fresh dill
2 tablespoons finely chopped fresh mint
2 tablespoons fruity olive oil

Salt the grated cucumber lightly to season it. Beat the yogurt with a wooden spoon until it is smooth and add it to the cucumber. Add the garlic, lemon rind and juice (if using), dill, mint and olive oil. Stir well, adding about 250 ml (8 fl oz) water, until it is the consistency of thick soup. Serve well chilled in small bowls, with a table full of *mezéthes*.

SCORTHÓZOUMI

GARLIC SOUP

In Greece, the third week of the Carnival period which precedes Lent is *Tirini* (cheese week), when *tirózoumi* (literally, cheese juice) is traditional fare. I call this version 'garlic juice', as garlic is its most distinctive ingredient.

SERVES 4

2-3 heads garlic – 3 is for the stout-hearted – cloves, peeled
1 tablespoon mountain thyme (page 16)
2 bay leaves
10 black peppercorns
175 g (6 oz) féta cheese,
or mizíthra or cottage cheese
250 ml (8 fl oz) thick yogurt
1 heaped tablespoon flour
2 medium-sized eggs
salt
4 tablespoons finely chopped rocket or watercress

KIRIA SOPHIA'S KITCHEN *My neighbour Kiria Sophia cooks on a wood-burning stove in a kitchen which has hardly changed in 200 years.*

In a soup pot, pour 1.5 litres (2 pt 8 fl oz) water over the garlic, thyme, bay leaves and peppercorns, and boil for 20-30 minutes. Strain the broth through a fine sieve, pressing firmly with a wooden spoon.

Return the broth to the soup pot and crumble the cheese into it. Beat the yogurt with the flour until smooth. This should prevent the yogurt from curdling in the hot soup. Continue beating while slowly pouring in a ladleful of hot soup. Pour all this back into the soup and stir over a low heat for 10 minutes.

Remove the soup from the stove. Beat the eggs until frothy and slowly add 2 ladlefuls of hot soup to them. Stir the egg mixture back into the soup. Taste and season with salt. Sprinkle each serving with a tablespoon of chopped rocket or watercress, and serve with crusty bread.

39

PIES, BREAD, PASTA AND RICE

The island landscape is sometimes harsh and its resources limited. These time-honoured dishes combine traditional staples with fresh produce to make delicious use of simple ingredients.

HORIÁTIKO PSOMÍ *above* (p. 48), HORTÓPITTA *left* (p. 45), KOULOÚRIA *right* (p. 49)

WHEN WE ARRIVE, the room which is the heart of the house has been transformed. The kilims are rolled up in a corner and the table in the centre of the room is draped with a clean white sheet, as is the bed against the wall. In one corner, the old bread-making cupboard stands open, revealing jars of flour, bowls, sieves and wooden utensils. The bread trough which is the actual top of the cupboard already holds the hard white flour which has been sifted with salt. The men have been sent away for the day.

Thespina makes a well in the centre of the flour and pours water into it. She works the water into the flour and kneads the dough for 10-15 minutes. Flour on her brow, she sits down to sip her coffee while one of her daughters divides the smooth, elastic dough into balls and covers the trough with damp muslin. After an hour's conversation over coffee while the dough relaxes, the rolling begins. Thespina places one of the dough balls in the middle of the well-floured, white-sheeted table; she flours her hands and the broomstick reserved for this function and begins by making three rolling passes over the dough. She turns it a few degrees clockwise and continues with the same progression of movements, keeping everything well floured. Every so often she flips the sheet of dough over the broom handle, lifts it and unfolds it onto the other side. Eventually the transparent filo nearly covers the table. It is about $^{1}/_{25}$th of an inch thick. Everyone takes turns rolling ball after ball of dough and placing the sheets of filo onto the sheeted bed, flouring between the layers. Later, great trays of baklavá will be assembled and baked in the outdoor bread oven which is Thespina's pride, in preparation for the arrival of relatives from abroad. A flaky, hot spanakópitta, spinach pie, will be our tribute.

Filo is said to have been invented by the Persians and adopted by the Arabs, who introduced it to the rest of the Mediterranean. Versatile and easy to use, it makes a vast array of pies, sweet and savoury, large and small. On a smaller, easier scale, you can make the same dough as we made at Thespina's with 350 g (12 oz) high gluten or strong white flour, 1 teaspoon salt and 125 ml (4 fl oz) water. Divide the dough into 12 small balls and roll out a circle 30 cm (12 in) in diameter. Stack these on a large kitchen towel or muslin. Use them immediately or store them by rolling

them in the towel and wrapping it in plastic. They can be frozen or refrigerated.

Not all pies are made with filo of course. There are many other pastries too and pies such as rizópitta (see page 43) are made with a familiar pastry crust.

Atheneaus boasted there were at least 72 different kinds of bread in ancient Greece, which must have included anything made of grain. Whatever the form, not a meal is served without it. Many special breads are also made for festivals. There is Christópsomo, Christmas bread full of nuts and raisins (see page 132); the brioche-like New Year's bread, vasilópitta, with a good-luck coin hidden inside; Lenten bread, lagána, flat and crusty; Easter bread, tsouréki, which is egg bread flavoured with the puzzling, fruity taste of machlépi, the kernels of a kind of cherry tree, or mastíhi (see page 14). Holy bread, antíthoron, is given after communion, and there are breads made of refined white flour or whole wheat and from semolina, barley, rye, maize and any combinations thereof.

When Thespina makes bread, her husband fills the beehive-shaped oven with small branches and twigs. The oven is ready when the fuel is reduced to ashes and the walls glow red. Thespina sweeps the ashes to the back of the oven and fills it with bread, sweets, stuffed peppers, píttes and a roast in the reverse order from that in which they must be removed.

Pasta has long been a favourite in Greece and there is a vast array of pasta dishes – some developed under the influence of the Venetians and Genoese, others which are, I believe, indigenous, such as the hilopíttes on page 51. For up to 500 years the Venetians controlled many of the major islands of the Aegean along with the Genoese. It was a fortunate culinary incursion which among other things left lamb or seafood pastítsio, a macaroni-based pie, as the traditional first course for an island wedding feast.

Today rice is so common in Greece that the delicacies of the Turkish pashas who used to rule Greece have become the favourite Greek grain dishes. Simple dishes of rice with chickpeas or tomato sauce are standard Lenten fare, while making a complicated rice dish with probable Byzantine origins, such as mussel pilaf, is considered a test of a good cook in Greece. Memorable pilafs made with lamb or game are served for grand occasions.

RIZÓPITTA ME TYRÍ

RICE AND CHEESE PIE

This recipe was given to me by a nameless woman in an Athens street market. I noticed the greying bun punctuating her head as she perused the stalls of food, looking like Athena returned to her city in skirt and sweater. We discussed the walnuts. She gave me this recipe and glided away. She must know the endless pleasure she gave that day.

SERVES 8

350-425 g (12-15 oz) plain flour, plus extra
for rolling
½ teaspoon baking powder
125 ml (4 fl oz) fruity olive oil
salt
1 small egg, beaten with 1 tablespoon water
1 tablespoon sesame seeds

CHEESE FILLING
350 g (12 oz) short-grain, or medium-grain
risotto rice
1 tablespoon olive oil
salt and freshly ground pepper
350 g (12 oz) féta cheese
350 ml (12 fl oz) thick yogurt
25 g (1 oz) flat leaf parsley, finely chopped
25 g (1 oz) fresh dill, finely chopped
40 g (1½ oz) spring onions, white and pale green
finely chopped
3 medium-sized eggs

Start by making the pastry. Sift the flour and baking powder together. In a saucepan bring the olive oil, 125 ml (4 fl oz) water and the salt to the boil, then remove from the heat. Beat the flour into the liquid, little by little, to make a pliable dough. Turn this dough onto a floured surface and knead for 10 minutes until smooth and elastic. Place in an oiled bowl, cover and leave for at least an hour to relax.

Grease a 20 cm (8 in) loose-bottomed or spring-release cake tin. Divide the dough into two unequal parts and roll out the larger piece to measure about 28-30 cm (11-12 in) across. Cover the base and sides of the tin with the pastry. Roll out the second piece large enough to cover the top, then put it aside on a piece of waxed paper.

To cook the rice for the filling, put 700 ml (1¼ pt) water in a heavy-bottomed saucepan with the olive oil and a pinch of salt and bring to the boil. Add the rice, stir, cover, and turn down the heat. Simmer until done – about 20 minutes.

Meanwhile crumble the féta into the bowl of a food processor, add the yogurt and process until fairly smooth. Add the parsley, dill and onion and process just long enough to incorporate them – barely more than a flick of the switch. Break one egg at a time into the bowl and process it before adding the next – again barely more than a flick of the switch.

Add this mixture to the cooked rice, season it and stir so they are well combined, and place in the prepared pastry case. Smooth the top, and cover with the reserved pastry round. Moisten the edges with a little water on your finger to ensure a seal, then crimp the edges attractively.

Cut two attractive patterns in the top – heart, crescent or leaf-shaped, using a shaped biscuit cutter, if you are uncertain of your carving ability. Lift up the cut-outs and move them over between the two spaces they left, so there are four shapes; two positive and two negative. Glaze the top with a little of the egg mixture and sprinkle with the sesame seeds.

Place on a baking sheet and bake in an oven preheated to 180°C (350°F, gas 4) for 60-70 minutes, until golden brown. Cool for 10-15 minutes, then remove the tin and serve. This pie is at its best served lukewarm, or at room temperature.

HORTÓPITTA

GREEN VEGETABLE PIE

This type of *pítta* used to be known as *sfungato* and was a speciality of the Italianate islands of Corfu and Zakynthos. It is good eaten hot or cold and travels well on picnics.

SERVES 4

125 g (4 oz) green beans, without strings
4 medium-sized courgettes, trimmed
125 g (4 oz) spinach, large stalks removed, washed
and finely chopped
125 g (4 oz) féta cheese, well crumbled
125 g (4oz) kefalograviéra cheese
or Parmesan, grated
2 tablespoons finely chopped flat leaf parsley
2 tablespoons finely chopped fresh dill
1 tablespoon finely chopped fresh mint
40 g (1½ oz) toasted breadcrumbs or
paximáthia (see page 10)
6 medium-sized eggs, well beaten
salt and freshly ground black pepper
1 tablespoon sesame seeds
1-2 teaspoons fruity olive oil

In a pot of boiling water, blanch the green beans and courgettes for about 4 minutes, or until *al dente*. Drain and chop them finely. Put the chopped vegetables in a large mixing bowl, and add the finely chopped spinach, parsley, dill and mint. Toss so they are evenly distributed. Mix the breadcrumbs, cheeses and eggs together and season well. Pour over the vegetables and stir until everything is well incorporated.

Use the olive oil to grease a baking dish of about 1.2 litres (2 pt), or a loose-bottom cake tin 20 cm (8 in) in diameter, and turn the vegetable mixture into it, smoothing the top. Sprinkle with sesame seeds. Bake in an oven preheated to 180°C (350°F, gas 4) for about 35 minutes, until the pie is golden and springy to the touch. Serve hot or cold, either from the dish or turned out of the cake tin.

WORKING IN THE FIELDS *Lush grass is cut in preparation for hay-making on Corfu.*

ARNÓPITTA

LAMB PIE WITH CURLY ENDIVE AND HERBS

This is a dish for a party or a picnic.

SERVES 6-8

1.5 kg (3 lb) boned shoulder of lamb, plus the bones
2.5 cm (1 in) piece of cinnamon bark
1 clove
10 black peppercorns
1-2 bay leaves
1 garlic clove
20 saffron strands, soaked in 50 ml (2 fl oz) boiling
water for 20 minutes
75 g (3 oz) plain flour

TO FINISH

700 g (1½ lb) curly endive, finely chopped
2 bunches spring onions, chopped with the greens
25 g (1 oz) fresh dill, chopped
2 tablespoons finely chopped fresh mint
5 medium-sized eggs, beaten
15 g (½ oz) pulverized paximáthia (see page 10),
or toasted wholemeal breadcrumbs
salt and freshly ground black pepper
125 ml (4 fl oz) liquid from the roast

To roast the lamb you need an iron or earthenware pot fitted with a tight lid. Cut the meat into large pieces and place in the pot with the bones, cinnamon, clove, peppercorns, bay leaves, garlic, saffron and its liquid. Mix the flour with enough water to make a sticky dough and with this seal the lid. Cook in an oven preheated to 180°C (350°F, gas 4) for 2 hours.

When you remove the top, you should find succulently tender meat and a fair amount of juice, which you should reserve. Remove the bones and cut the meat into reasonable-sized cubes or shreds. Mix with the endive, onions, dill and mint. Mix the eggs with the breadcrumbs, season with salt and pepper, and stir into the lamb mixture.

Turn into a well-oiled casserole, about 1.1 litres (2 pt), and drizzle with the roasting juices. Bake in an oven preheated to 190°C (375°F, gas 5) for about 30 minutes, or until just brown on top.

SPANAKÓPITTA NISTÍSIMI

LENTEN SPINACH PIE

This *spanakópitta* has no cheese or eggs, which are always included in the classic version known around the world. If you love green leaf vegetables, then you will revel in its pounds of luscious Lenten greens. Metaxia, who gave me this recipe, always includes the tender young leaves of wild poppies, an infusion of which the island women use to put cranky children to sleep. The pastry crust is rolled out very thinly and is a kind of rough-and-ready filo.

SERVES 8

*1.5 kg (3 lb) spinach, washed and large
stalks removed*
500 g (1 lb) curly endive
*2-3 bunches large spring onions, white and green
chopped together, about 250 g (8 oz)*
1 lemon
75 g (3 oz) flat leaf parsley, finely chopped
75 g (3 oz) fresh dill, finely chopped
1 teaspoon salt
freshly ground black pepper
5 tablespoons fruity olive oil
1 tablespoon rice or cracked wheat (bulgar)

PASTRY

200 g (7 oz) plain flour, plus extra for rolling
1 teaspoon sea salt
1 teaspoon baking powder
about 5 tablespoons olive oil
1 tablespoon sesame seeds

Start by making the pastry. Sift the flour with the salt and baking powder. Mix in about 75 ml (3 fl oz) water, a little at a time, until the dough is gooey, but not wet. Add 1 tablespoon olive oil, plus another teaspoonful, and a little more flour, if needed, to make a cohesive mass. Knead the dough for 5-10 minutes, until smooth and elastic. Cover it and set aside to relax for an hour or two.

For the filling, separate the curly endive leaves, so the vegetable will cook in the same time. Steam the spinach and endive together in a large pan, in the water clinging to the leaves, plus just an extra 125 ml (4 fl oz). Turn the leaves over occasionally, so they wilt evenly. When they are wilted, but not mushy, drain them in a colander, pressing firmly with the back of a wooden spoon to remove as much excess liquid as possible. (Reserve the liquid for use in soup, or drink with a squeeze of lemon juice, as the Greeks do.)

Sauté the spring onions in 2 tablespoons olive oil, until barely soft. Add a few tablespoons of water if they stick to the pan. Roughly chop the cooked spinach and curly endive and finely grate the zest from the lemon. Then toss the cooked vegetables with the spring onions, parsley, dill, lemon zest and 1 tablespoon lemon juice, salt and pepper, adding 3 tablespoons olive oil. Set aside until you are ready to fill the pastry.

Choose an earthenware or ovenproof glass casserole with 5-6 cm (2-2½ in) sides and about 1.7 litres (3 pt) capacity and brush the inside with oil. Divide the pastry into two unequal parts, and then again into halves. On a floured surface roll out one of the larger quarters of pastry. This should be large enough to fit into the dish and come up and over the sides – this should make it very thin. Fit it into the baking dish and brush it with olive oil. Do the same with the second larger quarter, placing it on top of the first, and brush again with olive oil.

Sprinkle the tablespoon of rice or cracked wheat over the bottom, to soak up excess juices, and fill with the spinach and herb mixture. Roll out the remaining two quarters of pastry to fit the top of the dish. Place the first on top of the spinach, brush with olive oil, then place the second on top of that. Prick the pastry with a fork in an attractive pattern and brush the entire top with olive oil. Sprinkle with sesame seeds. Bake in an oven preheated to 180°C (350°F, gas 4) for 45-50 minutes, until golden brown.

KOTÓPITTA

CHICKEN PIE

A *kotópoulo* used to be the word for a very small chicken, or what we would call a poussin, and *órnitha* was a normal-sized chicken. Today a *kotópoulo* is a chicken – any chicken. The name of this dish has been *kotópitta* as far back as I can trace, which means it must have been made with poussins.

This method of boiling meat with one set of spices, and then shredding and cooking it in another manner, probably came from the ancient Persians and spread through the early Islamic Empire to the oriental parts of the Mediterranean and as far away as India. The object was to create an exquisite mélange of tastes that didn't have to be chewed with effort to be enjoyed.

SERVES 6

2 poussins, 700-850 g (1-1¾ lb) each, or a
chicken 1.4 1.8 g (3-4 lb)
700 g (1½ lb) onions, finely chopped
3 tablespoons fruity olive oil
1 teaspoon honey
½ teaspoon freshly ground black pepper
1 pinch of nutmeg (¹⁄₁₆ teaspoon)
6 medium-sized eggs
125 ml (4 fl oz) chicken stock (see recipe below)
½ teaspoon rosewater
16 sheets filo pastry 50 x 30 cm (20 x 12 in) –
probably 1½ packets
1-2 teaspoons cracked wheat (bulgar)
175 ml (6 fl oz) olive oil
1½ tablespoon sesame seeds

POACHING LIQUID
100 g (4 oz) onion, chopped
3 garlic cloves
tops and leaves of 6-8 celery stalks
1 tablespoon black peppercorns
1 piece cinnamon bark, 4 cm (1½ in)
1-2 cloves
¼ teaspoon anise seeds
1 strip orange zest, about 5 cm (2 in) long
salt

Put the chicken(s) in a large pot with the poaching ingredients. Barely cover with water, bring to the boil, and cover tightly. Simmer very slowly for 45 minutes-1 hour – until the chicken is falling from the bones.

Remove from its juice. When the chicken is cool, remove all the flesh from the bones. Shred the chicken into bite-sized pieces, or even smaller.

In a heavy-bottomed saucepan sauté the onions in olive oil until they are burnished brown, but not burnt. Add little splashes of water, if necessary, to keep it from burning. This could take 15-20 minutes. Turn the heat way down, and add the honey, pepper and nutmeg. Beat the eggs with 125 ml (4 fl oz) chicken stock, and stir into the onions. Cook slowly, stirring, until you have a smooth custard. Remove from the heat and stir in the chicken and rosewater.

Keep the main pile of filo pastry covered with a damp tea towel. On a large oiled, or non-stick, baking sheet lay out one sheet of filo, brush it with olive oil and continue this process, until you have 6 layers. The filo may overlap the baking sheet a bit: don't worry.

Sprinkle the cracked wheat in the centre of the pastry, leaving a border of about 7.5 cm (3 in) all round. Spoon half the chicken mixture onto this. Lay 4 sheets of filo pastry over this, brushing each layer with oil, and top with the rest of the chicken.

Place 6 more layers of filo over the chicken, brushing each layer. Cut the edges of all the protruding layers, so they extend about 7.5 cm (3 in) around the pie. Brush the entire surface of the top layer with oil and roll up the edges. Sprinkle with sesame seeds. Bake in an oven preheated to 180°C (350°F, gas 4) for about 1 hour, until the pastry is glistening gold.

HORIÁTIKO PSOMÍ

COUNTRY BREAD WITH SEMOLINA
AND CORN MEAL

This is a typical country bread. To my knowledge, the only other place in the world where they make bread from semolina flour is Sicily, which was once part of Magna Graecia. Who knows who got it from whom? I learned to put *mastíhi* in it from Kiria Marina who makes it for her taverna in Vlichos. If you don't like the taste of *mastíha* or *oúzo*, throw a handful of coriander and anise seeds into the dough instead.

MAKES 1 LARGE OR 2 SMALL LOAVES

18 g (⅔ oz) dried yeast
75 ml (3 fl oz) very warm water
½ teaspoon sugar
*850 g-1 kg (1 lb 14 oz-2 lb) semolina flour or
strong unbleached flour*
250 g (8 oz) corn meal (polenta)
2 teaspoons salt
*1 piece mastíhi (see page 14) – ⅛ teaspoon –
ground to a powder with pestle and mortar, or
3 tablespoons mastíha liquor or oúzo*
½ teaspoon vinegar (if your water is hard)
50 g (2 oz) honey
50 ml (2 fl oz) olive oil
1-2 tablespoons sesame seeds

Sprinkle the dried yeast into the warm water and stir in the sugar. Mix together the smaller quantity of flour with the corn meal and salt in a large bowl.

Put the powdered *mastíhi* or liquor into a measuring jug and make up to 500 ml (18 fl oz) with warm water and vinegar, if needed. Stir in the honey and olive oil. Pour this into the flour, beating to make a sticky dough. When the yeast is frothy, and has doubled in volume, stir or beat it into the dough. Continue to stir, adding more flour as needed, until the dough becomes less sticky and more cohesive.

Turn out the dough onto a well-floured surface and knead until smooth, elastic and feeling like velvet. Add more flour as needed. Put the dough back into the oiled bowl, cover it with a damp cloth and let it rise until almost double in bulk – about an hour.

Punch down the dough and knead for another 5 minutes. Push it into a roughly ovoid shape, about 2.5 cm (1 in) thick, by holding your fists clenched and rocking the back of your knuckles back and forth. This squeezes out any over-sized air bubbles. Roll the dough back up like a rug, and pat into any shape you like – one or two loaves.

Place on an oiled or non-stick baking sheet. Cut a few diagonals across the top. Cover with a cloth and leave to rise in a warm, draught-free place for about 1 hour (for 2 loaves), until almost double in bulk.

OUTDOOR OVEN *Such beehive-shaped ovens, fitted with a removable iron door, are still in use on the islands.*

Almost is a key word here, as your bread will become rather flat if you let it rise too far. Sprinkle with sesame seeds.

Bake in an oven preheated to 180°C (350°F, gas 4) for 1¼ hours, for a large loaf, or 45 minutes for two small ones. The bread is done when the hot loaf makes a hollow sound when tapped on the bottom.

KOULOÚRIA

SESAME SEED RINGS

These are sold in the street in Athens and in every bakery in Greece, which is why most Greeks don't make them at home. But if you don't want to miss a common treat, you will have to make them yourself.

MAKES 12-15

40 g (1½ oz) sesame seeds
375 g (13 oz) plain flour, plus extra for kneading
¼ teaspoon salt
4 medium-sized eggs
4 tablespoons fruity olive oil

Start by toasting the sesame seeds. Put them in a frying-pan over medium heat. When you start to smell them, or see them turning golden, shake the pan until they are fairly uniform in colour. Remove the pan from the heat and empty it immediately, as the seeds go on toasting.

To make the dough, put the flour and salt in a large bowl. Beat together 3 of the eggs, with 4 tablespoons cold water and the olive oil and add to the flour. Stir with a wooden spoon until a dough is formed. Turn this out onto a well-floured surface and knead for 10 minutes.

Break the dough into 12-15 equal pieces and roll one into a rope or snake, about 2.5 cm (1 in) in diameter. Bend into a circle, pinching the ends together to seal. Beat the remaining egg, brush the top and sprinkle generously with sesame seeds. Repeat until all the dough is used, placing them on an oiled or non-stick baking sheet. Bake in an oven preheated to 190°C (375°F, gas 5) for about 25 minutes, until golden brown.

SPITIKÓ PSOMÍ YEMISTÓ

BREAD STUFFED WITH GREENS, CHEESE, PEPPERS AND OLIVES

This is a movable feast in truly *horiátiko*, or rustic style. It is simply what is left over from other meals, baked into a loaf of bread, so substitutes can be made, according to what you have on hand. My favourite Greek olives, *throúmbes*, are highly salted and should always be well rinsed in fresh water before using.

SERVES 6-8

2 sachets dried yeast, 15 g (½ oz) each

½ teaspoon sugar

450-600 ml (16-20 fl oz) warm water,
at body temperature

775-850 g (1 lb 7 oz-1 lb 10 oz) semolina flour
or strong unbleached flour, plus extra for rolling

150 g (5 oz) wholewheat flour

150 g (5 oz) mixed-grain flour
(a mixture of barley, rye and oats)

2 teaspoons salt

50 ml (2 fl oz) fruity olive oil

50 ml (2 fl oz) petimézi, grape must syrup
(see page 13) or molasses

FILLING

450-575 g (1-1¼ lb) curly endive or any greens
of your choice, steamed, drained and chopped

250 g (8 oz) roasted green peppers (see page 72),
from about 600 g (1¼ lb) peppers

250 g (8 oz) onions, chopped

3 tablespoons olive oil

1 teaspoon sugar

250 g (8 oz) throúmbes or any other Greek olive,
stoned and roughly chopped

175 g (6 oz) féta cheese

2-3 garlic cloves, finely chopped

15 g (½ oz) flat leaf parsley, finely chopped

15 g (½ oz) fresh dill, finely chopped

2 tablespoons finely chopped fresh mint

1 teaspoon rice or cracked wheat (optional)

Make the bread dough. Put the dried yeast in a cup with 125 ml (4 fl oz) hot water (just above body temperature, to your finger). Stir in the sugar and leave in a warm, undisturbed spot to 'prove'.

Mix the semolina flour or strong unbleached flour with the wholewheat and mixed grain flours, adding the salt. Pour onto a work surface, making a hollow in the centre. When the yeast is frothy and doubled in bulk, pour it into the centre, with the olive oil, *petimézi* or molasses and 250 ml (8 fl oz) warm water. Mix together to make a cohesive dough, adding more water as needed.

Knead the dough, keeping the work surface, the hands and the dough floured until the dough is velvety and elastic – about 25 minutes. Cover with a damp cloth and leave to rise until almost double in bulk – about an hour.

Make the filling, so it can cool before use. Sauté the chopped onion in the olive oil, adding little splashes of water if they stick. When burnished gold, sprinkle the onions with the sugar and cook until they caramelize. Assemble the greens and roast peppers, chopping them roughly. Drain all the cooked vegetables very thoroughly. If necessary rinse the olives. Make herbed cheese by mixing the *féta* with the garlic, parsley, dill and mint.

When the dough has risen, punch it down and divide into two slightly unequal pieces. Pat or roll each piece into a circle about 2-2.5 cm (¾-1 in) thick. Place the larger circle on an oiled or non-stick baking sheet. Cover both halves and leave to rise in a warm place for about 30 minutes.

If the filling ingredients are moist, sprinkle the dough laid out on the baking sheet with rice or cracked wheat. Layer the fillings, in order of preference, on the dough, leaving a border of 5-6 cm (2-2½ in) all round the edge.

Lay the second circle gently over the filling. Moisten the outer edges of the bottom and roll them round and over the edges of the top. Press to seal. Cut a few diagonal slits in the top for escaping steam and leave the dough to rise until almost doubled in bulk – about 1 hour.

Bake in an oven preheated to 180°C (350°F, gas 4) for 1 hour, or until there is a hollow sound when the hot loaf is tapped on the bottom.

HILOPÍTTES ME PÁPIA

HOME-MADE PASTA WITH DUCK

This is tiny rectangular-shaped pasta – *hílo* meaning thousand, *pítta* meaning pie – and in the villages the women still gather together to make it communally.

SERVES 4-5

1.8-2 kg (4 - 1½ lb) duckling
1 large onion, 200 g (7 oz), stuck with a clove
2 garlic cloves
1 sprig fresh thyme
1 bay leaf
25 g (1 oz) flat leaf parsley
tops and leaves of 6-8 celery stalks
¼ lemon
10 black peppercorns
salt
1.1 litres (1 pt 18 fl oz) water

HOME-MADE PASTA

600 g (1¼ lb) semolina flour or strong unbleached flour, plus extra for rolling
2 medium-sized eggs
1 teaspoon salt
125-175 ml (4-6 fl oz) goat's milk, or warm water, or a third egg
2 teaspoons fruity olive oil

GARNISH

strips of zest and juice of 1 lemon
2 teaspoons honey
1 tablespoon tahini (sesame seed paste)
salt and freshly ground black pepper
2 tablespoons sesame seeds, toasted
15 g (½ oz) flat leaf parsley, finely chopped

Make the pasta first. Place the flour in a mound on a work surface or piece of marble and make a well in the centre. Beat the eggs with the salt, 125 ml (4 fl oz) goat's milk (or water) and olive oil, then pour into the well. Pull the flour into the mixture to make a malleable dough, adding more flour or milk as necessary. Knead for 20-25 minutes. Place the dough in an oiled bowl. Cover with a damp cloth and leave for an hour or more, to let the dough relax.

Making sure you keep the work surface, dough and your rolling pin well floured, so nothing sticks, work with a quarter of the dough at a time. Roll it out to a rectangle thin enough to see through. Set the rectangle aside, flouring it well, so that you can safely place the next one on top of it. Roll the remaining dough the same way and pile on top. Let the rectangles dry for 20-30 minutes.

Cut the rectangles into 1 cm (½ in) strips, then into 1 cm (½ in) squares. The pasta can be cooked fresh, but is more often dried.

Spread these tiny pasta shapes on a tray and leave in the sun to dry. If you have no sunshine, dry them in an oven preheated to 140°C (275°F, gas 1) for 15-20 minutes. Once dried, they keep well in a glass or earthenware jar with a piece of cheesecloth or muslin tied over the top.

To cook the duck and serve the dish, you will need a pot big enough to hold the duck, vegetables and all the pasta, and water. Clean the bird, removing any excess fat. Put it in the pot and add 1.1 litres (1¾ pt) cold water. Bring slowly to the boil, skimming the surface. Add the onion, garlic, thyme, bay leaf, parsley, celery, lemon quarter, peppercorns and some salt. Simmer for 1 hour, until the duck is tender.

Remove the duck, strain the broth, and return this to the pot. Bring it back to the boil and add the *hilopíttes*. Cook them until tender – about 3 minutes if freshly made, 7 minutes for dried pasta.

Drain the pasta over a bowl to catch the broth, and put the *hilopíttes* on a large platter. Keep warm. Once more replace the broth in the pot. Cut the strips of lemon zest into julienne strips and add these, with the honey and tahini and season. Stir, then boil to reduce the liquid to about 475 ml (16 fl oz), then add the lemon juice.

Meanwhile skin the duck and remove the meat from the bones in large pieces. Arrange the meat on top of the *hilopíttes*. Pour the reduced liquid over the entire dish, sprinkle with sesame seeds and parsley and serve.

OLIVE GROVES ON SAMOS *(overleaf) The silvery green leaves of olive trees are counterpointed by the deep green of statuesque cypresses.*

ZYMARIKÁ ME REVÍTHIA KE PANZÁRIA

PASTA WITH CHICKPEAS AND CHARD

Chickpeas and pasta are old-time, poor people's food that deserve to be put before a king. There isn't a more satisfying or healthier meal.

I serve this simple vegetarian dish with sliced, fresh juicy tomatoes, sprinkled with *scorthostoúmbi* – garlic vinegar (*see page 25*) – olive oil and herbs, then lots of fresh fruit for dessert, along with the *melomakárona*, honey cakes on page 138.

This dish is commonly served during Lent, when cheese is forbidden in Greece. It is absolutely delicious with crumbled *féta*, however so you might want to pass around a bowlful. Take account of the saltiness of the cheese when seasoning, if you do.

SERVES 4-6

350 g (12 oz) chickpeas, soaked overnight in cold water
500 g (1 lb) chard or other greens, such as spinach, large stalks removed, washed and the leaves chopped
350 g (12 oz) mild Spanish onions, thinly sliced
2-3 tablespoons fruity olive oil
3 garlic cloves
finely grated zest of 1 lemon, juice of 1-2 lemons
25 g (1 oz) fresh dill, finely chopped
salt and freshly ground black pepper
250 g (9 oz) spaghetti or other pasta
a bowl of crumbled féta cheese (optional)

Drain the soaked chickpeas, put them in a saucepan and just cover them with cold water. Bring them to the boil and simmer for 10 minutes. Drain and rinse them, put them back into the pan, just covering them again with water. Bring to the boil and simmer 1-1½ hours until tender. Check them from time to time and add water if they are drying out. (They actually cook faster if you don't drown them, but you must be more careful to see they don't burn.)

In a fairly large, heavy-bottomed saucepan sauté the onions in olive oil until golden. Add the garlic, the grated zest of 1 lemon and the chickpeas. Season with pepper and cook over medium-low heat for about 5 minutes. Add the chopped leaves and simmer for about 5-10 minutes until these are tender. Add the juice of 1 lemon, chopped dill and season the dish. Stir, add the juice of the second lemon, if needed, and remove from the heat.

In a large pot of boiling water cook the spaghetti until *al dente* – about 8 minutes. Drain and transfer to a warmed serving bowl. Add the chickpeas and chard, toss and serve.

ACHIVÁTHES ME AVGOTÁRAHO

SHELL PASTA WITH DRIED FISH ROE

Avgotáraho – *botargo* as it is called outside Greece – is the dried eggs of the grey mullet. The entire egg sack of the fish is salted, dried, lightly smoked and covered in a layer of beeswax for protection. It has been esteemed since ancient times but, unfortunately, is now increasingly rare – and expensive. It is often eaten sliced with a drizzle of lemon juice.

I serve this simple but luxurious dish with a *horiátiki saláta* – a Greek salad, made of sun-ripened tomatoes, cucumbers, onion, green pepper, purslane, young dandelions and olives, tossed with a squeeze of lemon, olive oil and fresh mint.

SERVES 4-5

500 g (1 lb) shell pasta, or another shape
125 ml (4 fl oz) fruity olive oil
4 garlic cloves, finely chopped
2 teaspoons Seville (bitter) orange juice, or 1 teaspoon lemon juice and 1 teaspoon sweet orange juice
finely grated zest from ½ a Seville or sweet orange, or a lemon
1 teaspoon freshly ground black pepper
50 g (2 oz) flat leaf parsley, finely chopped
75 g (3 oz) avgotáraho, grated or 150 g (5 oz) smoked cod's roe, crumbled, or red caviar

Bring a large pot of salted water to the boil and cook the pasta until just tender – 8-10 minutes, according to the variety you are using. In the meantime, to make the dressing whisk together the olive oil, garlic, orange juice (and lemon, if using), orange or lemon zest and pepper.

When the pasta is done, drain it and place in a warmed serving bowl. Toss with the olive oil dressing. Sprinkle it with *avgotáraho* and chopped parsley and

A MASS OF GERANIUMS *These cheerful flowers add bright splashes of red and pink to many island courtyards and scented geranium leaves are invaluable in cooking.*

carefully toss again. If using crumbled cod's roe or red caviar, it looks prettier if you sprinkle them over the top of the individual pasta portions. Serve with a *horiátiki saláta.*

PILÁFI-LAHANIKÁ

VEGETABLE PILAF

Every family has its renditions of vegetable pilaf, depending on preferences and seasonal availability. It can be served *nistísimo*, on its own, for Lent, or as an accompaniment for any grilled or roast meats or fowl.

SERVES 6-8

350 g (12 oz) Basmati rice
15 strands saffron
150 g (5 oz) onion, sliced
1 medium-sized leek, cleaned and sliced
3 tablespoons olive oil
150 g (5 oz) waxy potatoes, diced
150 g (5 oz) carrots, sliced
150 g (5 oz) green beans, sliced
150 g (5 oz) courgettes, sliced
150 g (5 oz) tomato, skinned, seeded and flesh chopped
1 teaspoon salt
freshly ground black pepper
25 g (1 oz) flat leaf parsley, chopped
25 g (1 oz) fresh dill, chopped
1 teaspoon plus 1 tablespoon finely chopped fresh mint
1 lemon

Put the rice in a bowl, pour in cold water and swirl the rice and water with your hand. Drain and repeat this process until the water runs clear as you drain it. Return the rice to the bowl, fill it once more with cold water and leave to soak 20 minutes. Put the saffron strands to soak in 50 ml (2 fl oz) boiling water.

In a heavy-bottomed casserole fry the onion and leek in the olive oil over low heat until transparent. Add the potatoes, carrots, green beans, courgettes, chopped tomato, saffron and its liquid and sprinkle with the salt and some pepper. Stir, then cover and let them simmer for 5 minutes.

Drain the rice and spread it in an even layer over the vegetables. Pour in 700 ml (1¼ pt) water, then sprinkle with 15 g (½ oz) each chopped parsley and dill, 1 teaspoon chopped mint and the finely grated zest of ½ lemon. Cover and simmer for about 15 minutes, until craters form on top of the rice.

Remove from the heat, cover the top with a piece of cheesecloth or muslin (or a tea towel) and replace the lid. Put in a warm corner of the kitchen for 20 minutes for the rice to steam and for all the water to be absorbed. Turn out onto a warmed serving platter, so that the vegetables are on top. Sprinkle with the remaining chopped parsley, dill and mint. Drizzle with the juice of the lemon and serve.

SPANAKÓRIZO

SPINACH RICE

This simple dish is a Greek national favourite.

SERVES 4-6

1 kg (2 lb) fresh spinach
375 g (13 oz) onions, finely chopped
4 tablespoons olive oil
175 g (6 oz) medium-grain, risotto rice
25 g (1 oz) flat leaf parsley, finely chopped
25 g (1 oz) fresh dill, finely chopped
finely grated zest of 1 lemon, plus 1 teaspoon juice
salt and freshly ground black pepper

Wash the spinach thoroughly in cold water. Remove tough stalks and chop it coarsely.

In a large saucepan fry the onions in the olive oil over low heat until transparent. Add the spinach and a splash of water, and cook until the spinach wilts.

Add the rice, parsley, dill and lemon zest and season with salt and pepper. Add 400 ml (14 fl oz) water and stir. Cover and cook gently until craters form on the surface of the rice, about 15 minutes.

Remove the pan from the heat, place a piece of cheesecloth or muslin over the top and replace the lid. Put the pan in a warm place for 15-20 minutes. Stir, squeeze a little lemon juice over the top, and serve.

PRASSÓRIZO *above (p. 59)*, PILÁFI-LAHANIKÁ *below*

PRASSÓRIZO

SAFFRON RICE WITH LEEKS

SERVES 4-6

4-6 sun-dried tomatoes (see page 16)
20-25 saffron threads
1 kg (2 lb) leeks
4 tablespoons olive oil
½ teaspoon sugar
⅛ teaspoon freshly ground cinnamon
salt and freshly ground black pepper
175 g (6 oz) medium-grain, risotto rice
25 g (1 oz) flat leaf parsley, chopped
2 tablespoons chopped fresh mint

Cut the sun-dried tomatoes into little bits with kitchen scissors and put to soak (unless they are in oil) in a mortar with 50 ml (2 fl oz) boiling water. Put the saffron strands to soak in a cup in the same amount of boiling water.

Clean the leeks by removing the roots and the tough greens. Split them lengthways up the middle and rinse in cold, running water, being sure to remove the sand hiding between the layers. Cut into 2.5 cm (1 in) slices.

In a large saucepan fry the leek slices in the olive oil, sprinkling them with the sugar. Stir carefully, so as not to scorch them and cook for about 10 minutes. When they begin to soften, drain the water from the sun-dried tomatoes into the pan. Crush the tomato in the mortar with the pestle and add the pulp too. Add the cinnamon, ¼ teaspoon salt and some pepper, then the rice. Stir over the heat for about 2 minutes.

Add the parsley, mint, saffron with its soaking liquid and 450 ml (16 fl oz) water. Stir, cover the pan and simmer for 10-15 minutes, until craters form on top. Remove from the heat. Place a piece of cheesecloth or muslin over the top, replace the lid and put in a warm place for 15-20 minutes for the rice to steam and until all the water is absorbed.

CORFU FARMHOUSE *Burnt sienna hues, made by mixing powdered iron oxide with whitewash, distinguish this farmhouse.*

VEGETABLES AND SALADS

The abundance of luscious vegetables produced by the Greek soil and sun, combined with the fasting traditions of the Greek Orthodox Church, have created a deliciously varied repertoire of vegetable dishes.

HORTARIKÁ YEMISTÁ (p. 68)

THE ISLAND AIR IN SPRING is like a warm embrace. In the glow of this springtime welcome I wander up the mountain into secret fields guarded by sentinels of wild asparagus. Lying on a bed of hyacinths I munch the first wispy asparagus, as sweet and pungent as the field and spring itself.

There are many other wonderful wild things to eat in spring. Artichokes and cardoons are six hours' walk from where I live on Hydra, but all around are the tiny purple grape hyacinths that are eaten as a bitter spring tonic. It is an extraordinary experience staring into a plate of steaming wild flowers. Down by the sea grows *almíra*, glasswort, a feathery succulent which is pickled and then put away for summer salads that almost taste of the sea.

Every spring, when the field is tented with wild things, our neighbour, Naughty Noti, used to sneak through the undergrowth, moving stones, making little terraces that eventually linked up, making bigger terraces that became walls. He planted a tree here, and some vegetables there, working over many secret years. Then he went to the town registrar to claim the so-called abandoned land for his own.

He did this three times. And three times we bought back that which already belonged to us. After the third time we signed a contract by which we paid Noti for improvements made to our land, thus enabling us all to enjoy the fruits of his labour . . . staggering tomatoes, sweet baby cauliflowers, polished green peppers, the freshest courgettes with their bright yellow flowers which we stuff with a mixture of herbs and *féta* cheese for fritters. Dear Naughty Noti is no longer among us and I like to remember him as someone with his own special way of rearranging natural resources.

A good third of the year in the Greek Orthodox church is comprised of *nistía*, or fast days. If you are serious, *nistísima* (fast foods – not to be confused with McDonald's) do not include dairy products, eggs or fish with blood as they do in other churches. This leaves shellfish and mountains of vegetables and grains. *Nistía* is still widely observed, particularly on the islands, although less strictly in more urban areas. Thus Greece consumes more vegetables per capita than any other western country and I don't believe these figures include wild things.

And before healthfoods and fad diets, there was Lent, a solemn time of year when many people feel deprived. Quite honestly, I relish it. There are wonderful meals of meatless *moussaká*, stuffed vegetables, wrapped vegetables, stewed vegetables and raw vegetables. I cannot think of one vegetable that cannot be steamed or boiled and eaten hot or cold with olive oil and lemon all year. There are vegetable pilafs, vegetable *píttes* and pasta with vegetables. There are salads and pickles and earthy dishes of chickpeas, beans, peas and lentils. One of my favourites is artichokes *a la políta*, which means 'from the city', when the city was Constantinople. It is a stew of artichokes, carrots and potatoes seasoned with lots of fresh herbs, lemon and olive oil. *Briam* is a casserole striped with slices of potatoes, courgettes, onions, tomatoes and green beans. *Prassópitta* is layer upon layer of flaky filo filled with mouth-watering leeks. A plain dish of rice with chickpeas or tomatoes and olives is almost elegant in its simplicity. Some dishes in this book, such as the white beans with caviar, may seem extravagant, but to islanders various fish roes and their products have always been staples along with the beans, grains or pasta with which they were combined.

KOUNOUPÍTHI ME AROMATICÁ

CAULIFLOWER WITH FRESH HERBS AND VINAIGRETTE

Cauliflower in Greece is mostly white, sometimes purple and usually eaten boiled with oil and lemon or vinegar. As it is literally the flower of a cabbage, you are not obliged to throw away the leaves. If you don't see fit to use them in this dish, save them for soup.

If the cauliflower tastes strong and peppery when raw, it will have a strong taste, and stronger odour when cooked. If it is sweet and crunchy when raw – it will be delicious.

SERVES 4

1 medium-sized cauliflower
salt and freshly ground black pepper
2 tablespoons finely chopped parsley
1 tablespoon finely chopped dill
2 spring onions, finely chopped
1 scant teaspoon wine vinegar
¼ garlic clove, very finely chopped
¼ teaspoon oúzo or other anise-flavoured liquor
3 tablespoons olive oil

Break the cauliflower into florets, keeping tender and unblemished leaves with them. Blanch the florets in about 3.5 litres (6 pt) boiling salted water for 4-5 minutes, until barely tender. Remove and drain. If they are a bit too hard for your taste, proceed without rinsing. If they are just right (or a bit too soft), then rinse them in cold water to arrest any further cooking.

Place the drained cauliflower in a bowl and sprinkle with parsley, dill and onion. In a small bowl combine the vinegar, garlic, *oúzo* and season with salt and pepper. Whisk in the olive oil, pour over the cauliflower and toss. Serve hot or cold.

PRÁSSA TOU TAPSIOÚ

BRAISED LEEKS

Just as there are few modern savoury dishes without onions as an adjunct, so there were few ancient savouries which did not include leeks. Among other things, these vegetables were believed to give a sonorous singing voice.

SERVES 6-7

1 kg (2 lb) leeks
2 tablespoons finely chopped fresh mint
3 tablespoons finely chopped fresh dill
4 tablespoons finely chopped flat leaf parsley
salt and freshly ground black pepper
125 ml (4 fl oz) fruity olive oil

Trim the outer tough leaves of the leeks and cut to the point where the green turns a paler colour. Cut off the bearded root and split lengthways down the centre. Wash well, removing all the dirt hidden between the layers.

Place the leeks in a baking dish or casserole and sprinkle with the herbs, salt and pepper. Pour in the olive oil and 250 ml (8 fl oz) boiling water and cover the dish. Bake in an oven preheated to 180°C (350°F, gas 4) for 35-40 minutes, until tender.

KOLOKÝTHA YEMISTÍ ME LAHANIKÁ

WHOLE PUMPKIN FILLED WITH MIXED VEGETABLES

Greek pumpkins, which are actually edible gourds, are great misshapen monsters, usually weighing around 9 kg (20 lb). American pumpkins or jack-o-lanterns are actually better tasting, better sized and better shaped.

We have a pit in the garden where we sometimes cook entire meals, including this recipe, on a grand 20 lb scale for grand numbers. It is both festive and practical as a decorative, edible container holding all the cooked vegetables for a feast.

SERVES 8

1 pumpkin, 1.8-2 kg (4-4½ lb)
6 tablespoons fruity olive oil
175-200 g (6-7 oz) leek, including light green, washed and sliced
2 small turnips, peeled and diced
175-200 g (6-7 oz) green beans, trimmed and sliced
1 small fennel, sliced
175-200 g (6-7 oz) head cabbage, shredded
tops and leaves of 3-4 celery stalks, finely chopped
2 garlic cloves, finely chopped
½ teaspoon mountain thyme (see page 16)
salt
1 teaspoon honey
finely grated zest of ½ lemon, plus 1 teaspoon juice
1 teaspoon freshly ground black pepper
75 g (3 oz) cracked wheat (bulgar)
50 g (2 oz) flat leaf parsley, finely chopped
25 g (1 oz) fresh dill or mint, finely chopped
1-2 bay leaves with a handful of lemon leaves or a few cabbage leaves

Wash and dry the pumpkin. Cut a lid in the top large enough to get the filling in and out. Scoop out the seeds and sinews and discard. If the cavity is very small, scoop out a little flesh to accomodate the filling.

In a heavy-bottomed pot heat 3 tablespoons of olive oil and toss in the leeks, turnips, green beans, fennel, cabbage, celery and garlic, and sprinkle with

FRUIT AND VEGETABLE SHOP *The numerous fast days required by the Church make Greeks great consumers of vegetables.*

thyme and salt. Cover and sweat about 5-7 minutes – until the vegetables have lost some of their volume. Uncover and toss over high heat to evaporate some of the liquid, if there is much, being careful not to scorch the vegetables. Remove from the heat.

In a small bowl whisk together the remaining 3 tablespoons of oil with the honey, lemon zest and juice and pepper. Toss the vegetables with the cracked wheat, parsley, dill and this dressing. Spoon into the cavity of the pumpkin and replace the top.

Make a bed of bay and lemon or cabbage leaves in a roasting tin just large enough to fit the circumference of the pumpkin. Put the pumpkin on top of the leaves and bake in an oven preheated to 190°C (375°F, gas 5) for about 1½-2 hours – until the edible flesh is tender.

ANGINÁRES ME KOUKIÁ

ARTICHOKES WITH FRESH BROAD BEANS

The Mediterranean artichoke is smaller and much more tender than the great, hairy variety which grows in Brittany and Northern California. They can be eaten whole, including the choke, until nearly the end of the season. Most commercial artichokes are of the large globe variety, which need some attention before preparing this dish. If you can find the smaller Mediterranean variety, use them if they are very fresh – but I would always choose freshness over authenticity.

SERVES 8

4-8 artichokes, depending on their size
1 tablespoon lemon juice
125 ml (4 fl oz) fruity olive oil
1 kg (2 lb) broad beans in the pod, half shelled and half still in the shell
3 young leeks, split lengthways and washed, then cut into 4 cm (1½ in) pieces
salt and freshly ground black pepper
25 g (1 oz) flat leaf parsley, chopped
15 g (½ oz) fresh dill, chopped
2 tablespoons finely chopped mint
grated zest and juice of 1 lemon

Remove the tough outer leaves from globe artichokes and trim them so they are about 3-4 cm (1-1½ in) long. Remove the choke and trim the stem to about 2.5 cm (1 in), if the vegetable is small and soft, or remove stringy stems entirely. If the artichokes are very large, cut them in halves or quarters. Put them into a bowl of water acidulated with lemon juice, so they don't discolour while you work.

In a large flameproof casserole heat the olive oil and add the beans, artichokes and leeks, with salt and pepper. Sauté for about 5 minutes, add 250 ml (8 fl oz) water, cover and simmer for 20 minutes. Add the herbs, lemon zest and juice and continue simmering for another 5-10 minutes, until all the vegetables are tender.

MELITZÁNES TIS SKÁRAS

GRILLED AUBERGINES

I include Greece in the Middle Eastern culinary tradition which boasts over 1,000 ways to prepare aubergine. This recipe must be among the easiest and tastiest.

I have an unreasonable preference for the purple, or mottled banana-shaped aubergines. If you use the large purple ones, cut them in half, and then slice them.

SERVES 4-6

3-4 medium sized aubergines (oblong if possible), about 700-800 g (1½-1¾ lb), cut lengthways into 5 mm (¼ in) slices
salt
1-2 tablespoons olive oil
2 tablespoons vinaigrette
1 tablespoon finely chopped flat leaf parsley
1 teaspoon finely chopped fresh mint

Salt the slices of aubergine generously, arrange them on a large plate, and weight with another plate. Set aside for 30 minutes. Rinse them and dry between two towels, pressing well to remove bitter juice.

With a pastry brush paint the slices lightly with olive oil. Grill for about 2 minutes on each side, so they are tender.

Serve hot, drizzled with vinaigrette, and sprinkle with parsley mixed with fresh mint.

RÉVA ME VROÚVES

TURNIPS SAUTÉED WITH GREENS

Unless you grow your own turnips, you are not likely to be able to cook them with their own, lovely greens. Mustard greens are a good alternative, but you could try anything from kale and watercress to shredded Cos lettuce or spring greens. This is a delicious and easy accompaniment to any grilled or roast meat.

SERVES 4-5

1 garlic clove, cut in half
2-3 tablespoons olive oil
*4 turnips, 500 g (1 lb) together, peeled, halved,
and thinly sliced*
salt and freshly ground black pepper
grated zest and juice of 1 lemon
*350 g (12 oz) mustard greens or half and half kale
and watercress, roughly chopped*

In a large saucepan fry the garlic in the olive oil until brown, then discard. Add the sliced turnips and sprinkle with salt and the grated lemon zest. Sauté for 5 minutes.

Add the chopped greens and sprinkle with pepper and the lemon juice. Cover and steam for 1-2 minutes. Remove from the heat and leave covered for 10 minutes, to finish steaming.

HORTARIKÁ YEMISTÁ

STUFFED VEGETABLES

There are enough ingenious ways to stuff an array of vegetables to fill a chapter. Some are quite exquisite and some very basic, easy and tasty, like this one, which was devised by peasant women without ovens (this is still a quite common predicament in the Greek countryside today).

SERVES 6-8

3-4 large tomatoes
3-4 large onions, skinned
½-1 teaspoon salt
½-1 teaspoon sugar
lemon juice for sprinkling
3-4 peppers
3-4 medium sized courgettes
250 g (9 oz) long-grain rice
4 tablespoons fruity olive oil
700 g (1½ lb) minced lamb or beef
freshly ground black pepper
40 g (1½ oz) spring onion, white and tender
green chopped
25 g (1 oz) flat leaf parsley, chopped
15 g (½ oz) fresh mint, chopped
1 tablespoon rosewater
4-6 fresh lemon leaves, or cabbage or vine leaves
plus a strip of lemon zest
2 bay leaves

First prepare the vegetables. Stand the tomatoes on their stalk end and cut the top from the other end. Scoop out the pulp and seeds (reserving the pulp) and leave them to drain upside down. Cut lids from the onions. Scoop out the pulp with an apple corer or melon baller, leaving walls of about 0.5-1cm (¼-½ in), and reserve the pulp. Sprinkle the insides of the onions with salt, sugar and lemon juice.

Cut lids from the peppers and remove the pith and seeds. Sprinkle the insides with salt, sugar and lemon juice. Cut off the stalk end of the courgettes. Remove the pulp with an apple corer, leaving a wall of about 0.5-1 cm (¼-½ in) thick, and reserve. Sprinkle the insides with salt, sugar and lemon juice. Turn the tomatoes the right way up and sprinkle the insides with a little sugar.

Chop or mince the vegetable pulp in a food processor and reserve half the pulp for soup or some other purpose. In a large saucepan sauté the rice in 1 tablespoon olive oil until it becomes slightly transparent. Add the vegetable pulp and continue cooking until most of the juice is absorbed. Add the minced meat, with salt and pepper, and cook, stirring occasionally, until the meat is coloured. Remove from the heat, cool for 10-15 minutes and toss in the spring onion, parsley, mint and rosewater.

Loosely fill all the vegetables with the stuffing, leaving enough room for the rice to expand a little, and replace the tops.

Place the lemon or other leaves in the bottom of a wide stewing pot. Arrange the courgettes on them and drizzle over a little olive oil. Put all the other vegetables on top, drizzling each with a little olive oil. This should make 2-3 layers depending on your pot. Place the tomatoes on top so that they can be removed if they are done before the other vegetables. Pour 250 ml (8 fl oz) boiling water into the pot and throw in the bay leaves. Weight with a plate that fits inside the pot rim. Cover tightly and simmer, checking now and then that there is still a little water in the pot. After 30 minutes check the tomatoes and remove from the pot if they are done. Simmer the other vegetables for a further 15-30 minutes and serve hot or cold.

ÁGRIA MANITÁRIA ME YAOÚRTI

WILD MUSHROOMS IN YOGURT SAUCE

Imagine you might be wandering one day in a little valley we call 'Shangri-la'. You hear a woman call out 'Ékho manitarákia!' 'I have little mushrooms!' It is Kiria Barbara calling her brother to eat. If you show yourself, you will be invited to eat chanterelles or 'blushers', so named because they turn pink when the flesh is broken.

SERVES 4

700 g (1½ lb) wild mushrooms such as chanterelles,
or the same weight of cultivated mushrooms with
40 g (1½ oz) dried ceps or other dried
wild mushrooms
½ teaspoon salt
2 tablespoons cognac
100 g (4 oz) white and pale green of leek,
split lengthways down the middle, rinsed
3 tablespoons plus 1 teaspoon fruity olive oil
2 teaspoons fresh thyme or ½ teaspoon dried
mountain thyme (see page 16)
2 cloves garlic, finely chopped
100 g (4 oz) flat leaf parsley, chopped
15 strands saffron, soaked in 1 teaspoon
boiling water
175 ml (6 fl oz) thick yogurt
salt and freshly ground black pepper

Sprinkle the fresh mushrooms with salt. Let them sit for a few minutes and wipe with a damp cloth. In Greece mushrooms are very dirty and need soaking in salt water to loosen the dirt, and then a gentle wipe with a kitchen cloth. Slice if large.

Soak dried mushrooms (if using) in 175 ml (6 fl oz) boiling water with ½ teaspoon salt and the cognac, for at least 30 minutes. Drain the liquid through a damp cheesecloth and reserve. Rinse the mushrooms under running water to remove any grit, and chop roughly.

Slice the leek thinly and fry it gently in a large saucepan, in 3 tablespoons olive oil until tender. Add the mushrooms, thyme and garlic and stir for 1-2 minutes. Add the parsley (and reserved mushroom liquid, if using), stir and simmer for 20-30 minutes. When the mushrooms are tender, and most of the liquid has been cooked off, remove from the heat.

Beat the saffron strands and their liquid into the yogurt with 1 teaspoon fruity olive oil. Stir this into the mushrooms and serve hot. Or chill and serve with crusty country bread and steamed wild greens.

FASOLÁKIA FRÉSKA LÁTHERA

GREEN BEANS IN TOMATO SAUCE

The old way was to cook these beans in a large quantity of oil until they almost fell apart.

SERVES 6

3 tablespoons olive oil
1 large onion, 250 g (8 oz), finely sliced
½ teaspoon sugar
500 g (1 lb) tomatoes, skins and seeds removed
and finely chopped
4 sun-dried tomatoes (optional, for when the fresh
ones are uninspiring), in oil or snipped and soaked
in boiling water, pounded to a rough paste
3 garlic cloves, peeled and finely chopped
tops and leaves of 2-3 celery stalks, finely chopped
1 bay leaf, lightly crushed
$1/16$ teaspoon freshly ground clove
$1/16$ teaspoon freshly ground allspice
salt and freshly ground pepper
700 g (1½ lb) very fresh green beans,
trimmed and broken into halves or thirds

In a heavy-bottomed pot heat the oil and sauté the onion over gentle heat until transparent. Sprinkle with sugar and cook for a minute to caramelize, stirring occasionally. Add the tomatoes, garlic, celery, bay leaf, clove and allspice. Season and simmer uncovered for about 10 minutes until the sauce begins to thicken.

Stir the beans into the pot, cover and simmer for a further 15-20 minutes, until the beans are tender. (The timing depends on how fresh your beans are.) Serve hot or cold.

LAHANIKÁ YAHNÍ

VEGETABLE STEW

This dish is called a *yuvech* after the earthenware pot used for baking it, a *yahní*, or stew, if it is slowly stewed under a tight-fitting cover. I tend to use whichever method I have space for at the time. Some people like *féta* cheese crumbled into it when it is hot, or with a dollop of thick yogurt, when it is cold. It makes a main course for six, or a vegetable accompaniment for twice that number.

SERVES 6-12

500 g (1 lb) aubergines
350 g (12 oz) onions, sliced
4 tablespoons olive oil
½ teaspoon sugar
250 g (8 oz) red or green peppers, seeded and sliced
250 g (8 oz) courgettes, sliced into rounds
250 g (8 oz) fresh green beans (or okra, cleaned
– see page 23)
6 garlic cloves, chopped
500 g (1 lb) tomatoes, skinned, seeded
and finely chopped
4-6 sun-dried tomatoes (optional, for when the
fresh ones are uninspiring), cut into bits with
kitchen scissors and soaked in 50 ml (2 fl oz)
boiling water, or ready-soaked in oil,
or use 2 tablespoons tomato paste
125 ml (4 fl oz) oúzo or other anise-flavoured liquor
2 bay leaves
2 teaspoons fresh thyme or
½ teaspoon mountain thyme (see page 16)
¼ teaspoon freshly ground cinnamon
¼ teaspoon freshly ground cloves
½ teaspoon salt
freshly ground black pepper
25 g (1 oz) flat leaf parsley, chopped

Cube the aubergines and soak them in heavily-salted water for 30 minutes or more. Drain well and pat dry.

In a large heavy-bottomed pot (or flameproof casserole) fry the onions in 4 tablespoons olive oil over gentle heat until transparent. Sprinkle with sugar and caramelize them. Add the aubergine cubes and sauté until brown. Stir in the sliced peppers, courgettes, beans and garlic. Add more oil if necessary, and continue cooking at high heat, stirring frequently, for 5 minutes.

Add the chopped tomato and cook until a sauce begins to form. Then pour in the *ouzo* and season with bay leaves, thyme, cinnamon, cloves, salt and pepper.

Simmer, covered, over very low heat until the juices are absorbed. Alternatively bake the stew (transferring to an earthenware casserole or roasting tin if need be), uncovered, in an oven preheated to 180°C (350°F, gas 4) for 30-40 minutes. Stir in the parsley and serve hot or cold.

FASÓLIA ME BRIK

WHITE BEAN SALAD WITH RED CAVIAR

The scene is a fisherman's cottage on a lonely island promontory. A wicked west wind has been blowing for days and you are wickedly hungry. There are wild greens and herbs outside for the picking. Among the provisions in your *kellári* are *fasólia* and *avgotáraho* (*see page 12*). I have substituted caviar for the *avgotáraho* as it is more easily available.

SERVES 4-5

250 g (8 oz) haricot or other small white beans
½-1 teaspoon salt
100 g (4 oz) onion, finely chopped
1½ tablespoons olive oil
finely grated zest of 1 lemon, plus 2 teaspoons juice
½ teaspoon oúzo
15 g (½ oz) flat leaf parsley, finely chopped
4 teaspoons capers
8-10 lettuce leaves
175 g (6 oz) red caviar or salmon roe

Cover the beans by 5 cm (2 in) cold water and leave to soak overnight. Drain them, put them in a saucepan, cover with fresh water and bring to the boil. Cook for 10 minutes, then drain again. Return to the pan, cover again with water, and bring to the boil. Simmer, adding water when necessary, until the beans are tender but not breaking up – 1-2 hours, depending on the beans (haricots need just over 1 hour). Drain them and add ½-1 teaspoon salt.

Fry the onion gently in the olive oil with the grated lemon zest, until the onion is transparent. Remove from the pan and toss into the beans. Add the lemon juice, parsley and capers, stir and chill. (The dish can be made in advance to this point.)

Arrange lettuce leaves on individual salad plates, putting a scoop of beans on top. Sprinkle artfully with 40 g (1½ oz) caviar per serving.

FORBIDDING SEAS *A stretch of rocky coastline on Crete is a reminder of the harsher aspect of island life.*

MAVROMÁTICA ME DOMÁTES

BLACK-EYED BEAN SALAD WITH TOMATO AND BASIL

Black eyes flash at the sight of black-eyed beans. But unlike their Italian neighbours, the Greeks seldom use basil in the kitchen, although the ancients relished it and it grows on every windowsill and in every courtyard.

SERVES 4-5

250 g (8 oz) dried black-eyed beans
½-1 teaspoon salt
2 teaspoons wine vinegar
2 tablespoons fruity olive oil
1 tablespoon plus 1 teaspoon finely chopped onion
25 g (1 oz) flat leaf parsley, finely chopped
700 g (1½ lb) tomatoes, skinned, seeded and flesh chopped
2 tablespoons shredded fresh basil leaves
2 teaspoons finely chopped mint
pinch of sugar
salt and freshly ground black pepper
8-10 lettuce leaves

Cover the dried beans generously with water and leave to soak overnight. Drain, put in a saucepan and cover with fresh water, bring to the boil and cook for 10 minutes. Drain again, and cover with more fresh water. Bring to the boil and simmer, adding water when necessary, until the beans are tender – about 30 minutes.

Drain and toss with salt, vinegar, 1 tablespoon olive oil, onion and parsley then chill. (The recipe can be done ahead to this point and kept in the refrigerator for a day.)

Put the chopped tomatoes in a bowl with 1 tablespoon olive oil, the basil, mint, a pinch each of sugar and salt and some pepper and leave to macerate for 15 minutes. Arrange 2 lettuce leaves on each individual plate, place a scoop of bean salad on top and mask with the tomatoes. Alternatively, mix the tomatoes and beans together and serve in a large dish.

PIPERIÉS KE ROTHÁKINO SALÁTA

FRESH PEACH AND ROAST PEPPER SALAD

SERVES 8

20 fresh green peppers, about 2 kg (4-4½ lb), washed, cored, seeded and sliced about 4 cm (1½ in) wide
1 teaspoon sugar
4-6 tablespoons fruity olive oil
salt and freshly ground pepper
6 large fresh peaches, about 1.2 kg (2¾ lb)
CUMIN DRESSING
1½ teaspoons cumin seeds, toasted (see below)
¼ teaspoon cayenne pepper
salt
1 teaspoon lemon juice

In a large shallow roasting tin, spread the pepper slices so they are not more than 3-4 deep. Sprinkle with the sugar, olive oil, salt and pepper, and mix these in. In an oven preheated to about 190°C (375°F, gas 5) roast them uncovered for 1 or more hours, until the edges of some of them turn brown and crunchy. After the first 30 minutes, stir frequently so they don't burn or stick to the bottom. Don't be surprised by the substantial loss of volume.

Peel the peaches – if they don't skin easily, blanch them in boiling water for 1-2 minutes first. Stone and slice them. Toss with the cooled peppers – the volumes should be about equal.

In a dry frying-pan, toast the cumin seeds over a moderately high heat, until they pop a little and turn the colour of a grizzly bear. Shake the pan to avoid burning. If they smoke, they are burned and you must start again. Crush the toasted seeds and sprinkle them, mixed with cayenne and salt, over the salad. Toss with the lemon juice and a sprinkling of pepper and serve.

MAVROMÁTICA ME DOMÁTES *above*, PIPERIÉS KE ROTHÁKINO SALÁTA *below*

FAKÉS SALÁTA

LENTIL SALAD

Life on earth could be counted in lentils. They have sustained us for more than 8,000 years and their colour, taste and texture are those of earth itself. They are for all time and every season.

Here is a summer version of the timeless lentil. I often serve this with the peach and green pepper salad on page 72. They have become inseparable in the minds of many friends and family.

SERVES 8

500 g (1 lb) large dried brown or green lentils
1 pinch of bicarbonate soda (optional)
2-3 garlic cloves
175 g (6 oz) onion, finely chopped
4 tablespoons olive oil
1 teaspoon freshly ground coriander seed
½ teaspoon freshly ground cumin seed
¼ teaspoon cayenne pepper
¼ teaspoon freshly ground black pepper
salt
2 tablespoons wine vinegar
25 g (1 oz) flat leaf parsley, finely chopped
2 tablespoons finely chopped fresh mint

Clean the lentils: although they are packaged precleaned, I always pick them over to make sure there are no bits of rock disguised as tooth-breaking lentils. Just cover the lentils with water in a saucepan, adding a small pinch of bicarbonate of soda if your water is hard. Boil for 10 minutes.

Drain and rinse them. Return to the pan and bring to the boil in fresh water. Add the garlic, cover and cook 20-30 minutes, until tender. Check the water from time to time. The less water you cook them in, the faster they will cook.

Meanwhile, sauté the onion in 2 tablespoons olive oil until a well-browned rosy colour. Add the spices, salt and pepper and sauté for another minute. Drain the lentils and stir in the onions, with 2 more tablespoons olive oil and the vinegar, and chill. Just before serving, toss with the fresh herbs.

AVOCÁDO/NERÁNTZI SALÁTA

AVOCADO AND SEVILLE ORANGE SALAD

It is said that Athenian slaves could win their freedom by creating a pleasing new dish. If avocados and Seville oranges had been growing in the gardens of Athens at that time, I would have plied my masters with this winter salad – exquisite and rich in its freshness. It is a lovely accompaniment for spicy grilled lamb chops (*see page 106*) or grilled pork chops.

Any extra orange juice left over can be used to make a jar of special vinaigrette, using the bitter orange instead of lemon juice or vinegar.

SERVES 4

6 Seville oranges, with the zest of 1
1 tablespoon honey
8 – 10 Cos lettuce leaves, shredded
1 teaspoon olive oil
2 large ripe avocados
salt
toasted cumin seeds, crushed in a mortar with a pestle (see page 72)
1 pinch of cayenne pepper
1 teaspoon finely chopped fresh mint
4 tablespoons pomegranate seeds

Remove the zest from one of the oranges with a zester; or take off very thin strips with a potato peeler (being sure that there is no white pith) and then slice these into skinny julienne strips.

Put the honey with 3 tablespoons water into a tiny saucepan with the orange zest and simmer for about 5 minutes, until the zest becomes transparent. Boil to reduce the liquid to 1 tablespoon.

Taking each orange in turn, cut off the skin and outer membrane, exposing the inner flesh. (You need a very sharp knife for this.) Holding the orange over a bowl, pop each section out from between the membrane with the point of a sharp knife (you will be left with the membrane skeleton of the orange) and drop into the bowl, removing any seeds.

WREATH OF WILD FLOWERS *Such wreaths are traditionally made on May Day then hung on the door for good luck throughout the rest of the year.*

Toss the shredded lettuce with olive oil, some of the orange juice gathered in the bowl under the sections, and a pinch of salt. Arrange equal amounts of lettuce on four salad plates.

Pour off excess juice from the orange sections, toss with a pinch of salt and the reduced honey syrup. Spoon decoratively onto the lettuce. For each plate, cut half a peeled, stoned avocado into slices and arrange over the oranges. Sprinkle with a little orange juice, to help avoid discolouration, a pinch of salt and the cumin seeds and cayenne mixed together. Top with a pinch of mint and a tablespoon of pomegranate seeds. For maximum freshness, serve immediately.

POTATOSALÁTA ME THROÚMBES

POTATO SALAD WITH OLIVES, CAPERS AND PICKLED ONIONS

Potato salad is one of those dishes that varies according to the household and to who and what is in the kitchen. One of my favourite variations includes black-eyed beans.

The method of pickling onions is perfect for this or any other recipe and they are wonderful in a tossed green salad.

SERVES 4-6

1 kg (2 lb) waxy potatoes
salt and freshly ground black pepper
250 g (8 oz) onions, thinly sliced
2 tablespoons wine vinegar
½ teaspoon sugar
150 g (5 oz) Kalamata or throúmbes Greek olives
1 tablespoon capers
100 ml (3½ fl oz) fruity olive oil
1 garlic clove, finely chopped
25 g (1 oz) flat leaf parsley, finely chopped

Boil the potatoes in their skins in plenty of salted water until just tender. Run cold water over them, drain and leave until cool enough to handle.

To pickle the onions, place them in a saucepan just large enough to hold them, pour in the vinegar, 2 tablespoons water and sprinkle with sugar. Cover the pan and bring to the boil. Stir, cover and simmer for 1 minute. Shake the covered saucepan and put it aside for 5 minutes to steam.

Peel and slice or roughly dice the potatoes and place in a serving bowl. Sprinkle with the olives, capers and pickled onions – with their juice – olive oil, garlic and parsley. Toss and season to taste.

FISH AND SHELLFISH

The waters lapping the islands yield a catch of great diversity – from huge octopus, tuna and sea bass to red mullet, tiny squid and needlefish – and the methods of cooking them are just as legion.

LITHRÍNI PLAKÍ (p. 84)

A GREAT HEAT HAZE DESCENDS over the island in summer. The once azure skies turn the colour of bleached bones strewn across a desert. It is difficult to see. A walk through the town at midday is like a soundless stroll through a deserted town in hell. The weeds that sprang up between the paving stones in spring are so dry that they crumble beneath your feet. Dogs and cats lie prostrate under tables.

The town begins to stir again by early evening, and by nightfall it is resurrected. Those who don't have gardens or courtyards pull their tables, chairs and little grills into the streets. Children are out playing when they would be going to bed in cooler countries. The slightest breeze creates a carnival air, while neighbour offers neighbour a fish or piece of octopus from his or her grill – called a *foufoú* because one must blow on them, making a *foufoú* sound, to get them started. Down by the sea, the tavernas hiss with the smell of scorched sea – fresh fish on the *foufoú*. Summer nights and grilled fish are inseparable.

Lent, too, is another time when seafood is indispensable. Everyone usually spends the first day of Lent – a normally windy day in February – outside picnicking and flying kites. As well as meat, milk, and eggs, fish with blood are not allowed during this time by the Greek Orthodox church, so a 'Clean Monday' picnic traditionally includes sea urchins, oysters and cockles, all fresh from the sea, dressed only with a squeeze of freshly picked lemon. There are plenty of pickled vegetables and *taramosaláta* with *lagána*, the flat bread made specially for this day. And there is Cos lettuce salad with lots of spring onions and fresh herbs. Prawn and crab might be included. The rest of the crustaceans and bivalves, including cuttlefish, squid, octopus, spiny lobster, mussels and all fish roe products are all consumed in quantity during this period. Octopus hanging on a line like laundry used to be a common island sight. They were being air-dried before being stored for fasting days.

There is a cave around the back of the island of Hydra into which, if you are quiet enough, you can swim without disturbing the turquoise-feathered kingfishers that make their nest there. The sandy sea bottom is more sparsely carpeted with sea grasses than it used to be and the sea urchins, although they are still delicious, grow fewer every year, a sure sign that our pristine waters are threatened, as elsewhere in the Aegean and Mediterranean. My friend Argiris, who is a fisherman, tells me that he has seen ten species of fish disappear from the Saronic Gulf in the course of the last ten years.

I hope our grandchildren will not have to mix amino acids and enzymes in testtubes in an attempt to approximate the tastes and smells described in 'old-fashioned' cookery books like this one. I wish them the unimaginable thrill of seeing dolphins organizing their games, of touching a brilliant star fish or tasting a simple fresh fish.

I never met a fresh fish I didn't like nor a less-than-fresh one whose acquaintance I cared to make. If a fish doesn't stare back at you with shining, clear eyes, pass him up. If he has been filleted, his flesh should be firm and bouncy, like a baby's, when you poke him with your finger – not like an octogenarian's arm where a light squeeze would leave tracks.

If you live near the sea, any of the dishes in this chapter can be made with any of the fresh fish available. Likewise, if you live inland, make them with lovely freshwater fish. It is the spirit of Greek island cooking to make the best of what there is available. I have varied the methods and ingredients so that, with some minor alterations, you could theoretically use the same fish in every recipe in this chapter and never find your diet monotonous.

GARITHÓSOUPA ME SCORTHALIÁ

PRAWN AND RED PEPPER SOUP WITH ALMOND-GARLIC SAUCE

The last time I ate prawns straight from the sea, fishermen dumped them straight from their nets onto embers that glowed across a moon-dark beach, in another part of the Mediterranean, over 25 years ago. Perhaps it was time, place and youth that created a delicious memory I never expect to taste again.

You are best advised to buy fresh or flash-frozen uncooked prawns (the latter are frozen on the prawn boats and are as fresh as we can hope for). Some fishmongers have a habit of thawing the flash-frozen creatures and selling them as fresh. It is better to buy them frozen and thaw them yourself.

SERVES 4-5

750 g (1½ lb) large raw prawns with heads, peeled
450 ml (16 fl oz) Samos or other muscat wine
1 bay leaf
1 sprig rosemary
1 small hot red chilli
1 strip thinly pared lemon zest
salt
350 g (12 oz) red peppers
250 g (8 oz) onions, thinly sliced
2-3 tablespoons olive oil
1 garlic clove, finely chopped
tops and leaves of 2-3 celery stalks, chopped
2 tablespoons finely chopped fresh mint or basil
4-5 pieces paximáthia, bread rusks (see page 10),
or a piece of toasted wholemeal bread per person
Scorthaliá (see below), to serve

Put the prawn peelings, wine, 900 ml (1 pt 12 fl oz) water, bay leaf, rosemary, chilli and lemon zest in a soup pot and add salt. Bring to the boil and simmer, uncovered, for 20 minutes. Strain through a colander lined with damp cheesecloth or muslin.

Spear the peppers on a carving fork or skewer and hold over a flame until the skin bubbles, turning them round. (You can grill them, if you don't cook on gas.)

Put them into a paper or plastic bag, seal it and leave for 5-10 minutes. Peel off the skin and remove the stem and seeds. Slice half the peppers into thin strips and reserve. Purée the remaining pepper in a food processor, or pound in a mortar with a pestle.

In a flameproof casserole, fry the onions in the oil over low heat until transparent. Add the garlic, celery and red pepper and simmer for 5-10 minutes. Chop the prawns coarsely and add to the pan with the pepper purée. Simmer 1-2 minutes – until the prawns turn pink. Add the fish stock and heat through. Adjust the seasoning then sprinkle with mint or basil.

To serve spread a *paximáthi* with *scorthaliá* and place it in the bottom of a soup plate. Ladle the soup over.

SCORTHALIÁ

ALMOND-GARLIC SAUCE

This versatile sauce is commonly made just with bread or mashed potatoes. It is used for fried fish – particularly salt cod or shark – and for boiled vegetables, hot or cold. Try it with hard-boiled eggs, or swirled into any soup or stew that needs a spark.

ABOUT 8-10 SERVINGS

6-8 garlic cloves
½ teaspoon salt
150 g (5 oz) almonds, blanched and finely ground
50 g (2 oz) stale breadcrumbs, soaked in water
and squeezed dry
175-250 ml (6-8 fl oz) fruity olive oil
juice of 1 large lemon

Pound the garlic with the salt in a mortar until you have a smooth paste. Add the almonds and breadcrumbs and continue pounding until smooth. A food processor can be used, but you may need to add a tablespoon or more cold water to the almonds, so that the oil doesn't separate from them. (I prefer the mortar and pestle.) Beat in the olive oil by droplets, as for mayonnaise, to make a thick creamy emulsion. Beat in 2-3 tablespoons lemon juice and taste for salt.

KAKAVIÁ

FISH SOUP WITH VEGETABLES

A *kakávin* was an ancient stew pot carried on the boats of Greek fishermen all the way to Massilia, modern Marseilles, which they founded. It is the grandmother of the French *marmite*. In it one can put five different kinds of rockfish coming from the Mediterranean: the *scorpios* or scorpion fish is everyone's favourite. The others – *mylokopi, lychnos, sparos* and *drakena* – are the corb, star-gazer, annular bream and weever. They make good soup because they taste good and stay intact when boiled, which should be a criterion when looking for substitutes. Try salmon, hake, fresh cod, turbot, mackerel or any combination thereof.

If you are using scorpion fish, it is a good idea to cut the points from the spines with kitchen scissors before you proceed to clean and scale it.

In common with other fish dishes this is often served in two courses – the soup first, then the fish which was cooked in it. I prefer to serve them together and it makes a main course with bread and a huge salad.

SERVES 6-8

*2 kg (4½ lb) rascasse, scorpion or other
bony soup-fish with heads, scaled, gutted, washed
and cut into large chunks*

500 g (1 lb) onions, chopped

250 g (8 oz) leeks, washed and the white chopped

4 tablespoons fruity olive oil

50 strands of saffron

250 g (8 oz) carrots, diced

tops and leaves of celery stalks, chopped

*1 kg (2 lb) tomatoes, skinned, seeded
and finely chopped*

4 garlic cloves, finely chopped

1 small hot red dried chilli

*1 tablespoon fresh thyme or
1 teaspoon dried mountain thyme (see page 16)*

2 bay leaves

*finely grated zest of 1 Seville orange, plus
juice, or of ½ lemon and ½ sweet orange*

50 ml (2 fl oz) oúzo or other anise-flavoured liquor

2 tablespoons finely chopped fresh mint

100 g (4 oz) flat leaf parsley, finely chopped

In a flameproof casserole, fry the onions and leeks gently in the olive oil until translucent. Meanwhile pour 125 ml (4 fl oz) boiling water over the saffron strands in a cup.

Add the carrots, celery, tomato flesh, garlic, chilli, thyme, bay leaves and orange zest to the pan and simmer for about 10 minutes, until the sauce begins to

thicken. Add the *oúzo* and 1.2 litres (2 pt) water. Simmer another 20 minutes.

Stir in the mint and the saffron with its soaking liquid. Gently add the fish, and simmer 5-10 minutes until the fish is done, but not falling off the bones.

Add the parsley and orange (and lemon) juice and serve with crusty country bread.

PASTEL SHADES *The lime green and vibrant pink colours of these fishing boats sing out against a deep blue sea.*

CHURCH ON MILOS *(overleaf) One of the quintessential images of Greece – dazzling white against electric blue – is indeed to be found everywhere on the Cyclades islands.*

81

SOUPIÉS ME SPANÁKI

CUTTLEFISH OR SQUID WITH SPINACH

The differences between cuttlefish and squid are more apparent to native fishermen and marine biologists than to the rest of us. The important thing for the cook to know about these tasty creatures is that they are tough unless you cook them for 3 minutes or less (deep-fry or stir-fry), or more than 20 minutes. Anything in between results in rubber. The cuttlefish and squid in Greece have their ink sacs intact because they are line-caught – net-caught fish expel their ink as a reaction to being caught. Do try to use fish with ink sacs if at all possible, but this is still a very tasty dish if you have to make it without.

SERVES 6-8

1 kg (2 lb) small cuttlefish or squid,
with their ink sacs intact if possible
1 tablespoon oúzo or other anise-flavoured liquor
250 g (8 oz) mild Spanish onion, finely chopped
3 tablespoons olive oil
2 garlic cloves, finely chopped
350 g (12 oz) tomatoes, skinned, seeded
and flesh finely chopped
2 sun-dried tomatoes (in oil or snipped and soaked
in boiling water), pounded to a paste,
or 2 teaspoons tomato paste
15 g (½ oz) flat leaf parsley, finely chopped
15 g (½ oz) fresh dill, finely chopped
250 ml (8 fl oz) red or white wine – I use
either, depending on my mood
salt and freshly ground black pepper
500 g (1 lb) spinach

To clean the cuttlefish or squid, use the heads to pull the viscera out of the bodies. Make a cut above the eyes to free the tentacles, and keep these with the bodies. Look for the ink sacs in the viscera: the ink sac is a small bag with a silvery outside. Separate them, without breaking them, and put the sacs into a small sieve. Discard the rest.

Remove the 'skeletons' from the bodies. Cuttlefish have a thick but light white one, which may need cutting free, while the transparent quill in squid usually pop out when they are flexed. Peel the mottled skin off the outside of the bodies   salted fingers help. Wash inside and out and cut into bite-sized pieces.

Set the sieve with the ink sacs over a small bowl or cup, crush the sacs with the back of a spoon, extracting as much ink as possible. Pour in the *oúzo* and continue crushing until you have collected every available drop. Put the ink into the refrigerator until needed.

In a flameproof casserole fry the onions in the olive oil gently until transparent. Add the cuttlefish or squid pieces and continue frying for 5 minutes. Add the garlic, chopped tomato and tomato paste, parsley, dill and wine, season and simmer for 30 minutes.

Meanwhile wash the spinach, discarding thick stalks, and shred the leaves. When the 30 minutes is up, stir the spinach and the ink into the pan. Simmer for another 10 minutes. Serve with steamed rice or home-made pasta, *hilopíttes (see page 51).*

LITHRÍNI PLAKÍ

SEA BREAM BAKED WITH TOMATOES AND OLIVES

The cauliflower salad on page 63 or steamed courgettes with lemon juice and olive oil drizzled over them both make good accompaniments for this splendid baked fish.

For the sea bream you could substitute cod, red snapper, halibut, or even shark or tuna. It all depends on your taste and on what is available. A general rule of thumb for most of these fish is to cut very large ones into slices or steaks (or you can buy them already cut from your fishmonger). A medium-sized fish should be slashed in two or three places on each side, inserting a slice of garlic into each slash. Leave small fish whole.

If the fishmonger hasn't cleaned and scaled the fish, you can do so by holding it under running water and scraping off the scales with a knife, going from the tail towards the head. Holding the fish by the back of the head, insert your left thumb (if you are right-handed) under the left gill. Make a slit up the belly, to just below the gills. Insert the point of the knife sideways into the space in the jaw (just below the bottom teeth) and slit. Place your right index and middle fingers into the slit below the teeth and make a swift, hard jerk downwards, pulling out the gills and guts together in one movement.

SERVES 6

6 fish steaks, about 200 g (7 oz) each,
or 3 medium-sized fish (600 g [1 lb 6 oz] each
before cleaning), scaled and gutted
350 g (12 oz) onions, thinly sliced
4 tablespoons fruity olive oil
1 teaspoon honey
500 g (1 lb) tomatoes, skinned, seeded
and flesh chopped
4-5 garlic cloves, finely chopped
1 bay leaf, crushed
¼ teaspoon mountain thyme (see page 16)
2 tablespoons orange juice
2 tablespoons oúzo or other anise-flavoured liquor
salt and freshly ground black pepper
100 g (4 oz) Kalamata olives,
stoned and roughly chopped
2 tablespoons capers
40 g (1½ oz) fennel tops, finely chopped

Wash and prepare your choice of fish and arrange it in a single layer in an oiled baking dish. In a heavy frying-pan fry the onions in the oil over low heat until translucent. Add the honey, chopped tomato, garlic, bay leaf, thyme, orange juice and *oúzo* and season with pepper. Cover and simmer until the sauce begins to thicken – about 10 minutes.

Stir in the olives, capers and fennel and pour over the fish. Bake in an oven preheated to 180°C (350°F, gas 4) for about 30 minutes. Taste the sauce and add salt carefully, as both the olives and the capers are quite salty. Serve with great chunks of crusty bread to soak up the sauce.

SCOUMBRÍ ME AROMATICÁ
MACKEREL WITH HERBS

I like this with plain steamed Basmati rice and a tomato and dandelion salad.

SERVES 4

4 mackerel, about 350 g (12 oz) each
(uncleaned weight), gutted
1 lemon
salt and freshly ground black pepper
350 g (12 oz) onions, sliced
4 tablespoons olive oil
6 lemon leaves or cabbage or vine leaves
2 sprigs of thyme
250-350 ml (8-12 fl oz) fish stock or herb broth
(see page 37), hot
2 tablespoons plain flour
100 g (4 oz) flat leaf parsley, finely chopped
50 g (2 oz) fresh dill, finely chopped
2 tablespoons finely chopped fresh mint
1 tablespoon lemon juice

Wash the fish and blot dry inside. Sprinkle with lemon juice, salt and pepper inside and out and reserve.

In a heavy frying-pan fry the onions gently in 2 tablespoons olive oil until they are transparent. Line an oiled baking dish (the right size for the mackerel) with the lemon or other leaves and make a bed of onions over them. Place 2 sprigs of thyme on the onions and the fish in one layer over everything. Pour over enough hot fish stock or herb broth to barely cover. Cover with foil and bake in an oven preheated to 180°C (350°F, gas 4) for 30 minutes.

Meanwhile heat 2 tablespoons of olive oil in a saucepan, using a wooden spoon to stir in the flour to make a smooth paste. When the fish is ready, remove it to a warmed platter. Drain off the hot stock from around it and stir into the flour. Simmer, stirring occasionally, until the sauce coats the back of the spoon. Add the parsley, dill and mint and stir. Season with lemon juice to taste (about 1 tablespoon), adding salt and pepper and simmer for 5 minutes.

Mask the fish lightly with herb sauce. Serve the rest of the sauce in a jug.

BARBOÚNIA SE KLIMATÓFILA

RED MULLET IN VINE LEAVES

The Greeks have always esteemed the *barboúnia* or red mullet, but never as much as the Romans, who are reputed to have paid the equivalent of 4 pair of oxen for 1.5 kg (3½ lb) of red mullet. Before you have to trade your house, car or pets for these beautiful little redheads, remember this recipe is also good with fresh sardine or herring.

It is delicious accompanied by any of the vegetable and rice dishes in the book.

SERVES 4-6

12 fresh red mullet, 100 g (4 oz) each (uncleaned weight), scaled and gutted
24 vine leaves
salt
12 pieces fresh fennel tops
12 strips fresh lemon zest, from 2-3 lemons
2 tablespoons olive oil

FENNEL AND CAPER LEMON SAUCE

125ml (4 fl oz) fruity olive oil
1 tablespoon fresh lemon juice
2 teaspoons fresh fennel top, finely chopped
2 teaspoons chopped capers

If you are using fresh vine leaves, remove the tough part of the stem, blanch in boiling water for about 4 minutes and drain. If you are using vine leaves preserved in brine, rinse them in cold water and drain.

Rinse, pat dry and salt and pepper the cavity of each fish, placing a sprig of fennel and a strip of zest inside each one. Brush the outside with olive oil. Place one fish on two overlapping vine leaves. Roll it up, tucking in the sides after the first turn. Tie with a piece of grass, or string, if necessary.

Grill for 8-10 minutes. It is nice if you have a few branches of aromatic herbs to throw on the charcoal.

In the meantime make the sauce. Whisk together the olive oil, lemon juice, chopped fennel and capers. Serve the fish in their packets with the sauce, which is called *latholémono*, in a separate bowl.

BARBOÚNIA ME PRÁSSINA STAFÍLIA

RED MULLET IN SOUR GRAPES

Not having yet been introduced to the lemon, or any other citrus fruit, the ancients were in the habit of using sour grapes to lend fruity piquancy to their food. This dish of red mullet is inspired by that forgotten habit.

SERVES 4

8 red mullet, about 100 g (4 oz) each (uncleaned weight), scaled and gutted
1 medium-sized leek, washed and white finely chopped
3 tablespoons olive oil
800 g (1¾ lb) sour green grapes, preferably seedless
1-2 teaspoons honey (depending on the sourness of the grapes)
2 tablespoons lemon juice (optional) for use if the grapes are not sour enough
salt
½ teaspoon freshly ground pepper
125 ml (4 fl oz) white wine
3 tablespoons finely chopped fresh dill

If you don't have a frying-pan big enough to hold all the fish in one layer with the sauce, use a large shallow flameproof casserole. In it fry the leeks gently in the olive oil. Add the grapes, honey, wine, lemon juice if using, and salt and pepper, and simmer for 10 minutes.

Arrange the fish in the pan, carefully spoon some of the sauce over them and cover with a lid, foil or a baking sheet. Simmer for about 10 minutes. Sprinkle with fresh dill and serve straight from the pan, with crusty bread and braised leeks.

BARBOÚNIA SE KLIMATÓFILA

XYFÍAS ME KORÓMILA PLAKÍ

SWORDFISH STEAKS WITH GREENGAGE SAUCE

Imagine you are in a garden, overlooking the moonlit red-tiled top of an island town. The 'wine dark sea', as Homer called it, is glowing and the company is moonstruck. To the table comes a platter, luscious with swordfish from the sea below, smothered in plums from the tree above.

Any fresh tart plums will do, but greengages are plentiful in Greece and on the islands, as they can be grafted onto wild almond trees.

SERVES 4

4 swordfish steaks, about 200 g (7 oz) each
salt and freshly ground black pepper
3 tablespoons fruity olive oil
250 g (8 oz) onions, thinly sliced
1 teaspoon honey
2 garlic cloves, finely chopped
500-600 g (1-1 lb 6 oz) greengages or other plums,
stoned and quartered
25 g (1 oz) fresh fennel tops or dill, chopped
1-2 lemons, in wedges to serve

Salt and pepper the swordfish steaks. Arrange in one layer in an oiled roasting tin and drizzle with 1 tablespoon olive oil. In a heavy frying-pan fry the onions gently in the remaining 2 tablespoons olive oil until transparent. Add the honey and stir until it caramelizes. Stir in the garlic and the greengages (or plums) and simmer for 5-10 minutes. Add the fennel or dill and season with salt and pepper.

Scoop the plums and juice into the roasting tin round the fish. Bake in an oven preheated to 180°C (350°F, gas 4) for about 30 minutes. Swordfish is done when it turns opaque and the flesh feels firm. Transfer to a warmed platter or individual plates and garnish with lemon wedges. I serve this with plain rice or boiled cracked wheat.

GÓPES ME KARITHÓSALTSA

BOGUE (OR TROUT) IN WALNUT SAUCE

Gópes are considered the lowliest fish in the Aegean – probably because they are plentiful – although I prefer them to red mullet. Trout is a good substitute.

SERVES 4-6

1.4 kg (3 lb) bogue or trout fillets, or any other
delicate-flavoured fish
4-5 tablespoons crumbs from ground
paximáthia (see page 10), or stale wholemeal
breadcrumbs, plus about 250 g (8 oz) for rolling
2-3 medium-sized eggs, beaten
olive oil for frying
50 ml (2 fl oz) scorthostoúmbi, garlic vinegar
(see page 25)
125 ml (4 fl oz) dry white wine
½ teaspoon honey
75 g (3 oz) walnuts, well chopped
25 g (1 oz) flat leaf parsley, finely chopped
½ teaspoon freshly ground pepper
salt
additional walnuts to garnish

Chop the fish roughly then squeeze in your hand to remove excess liquid. Take bunches of chopped fish and press into balls about 5 cm (2 in) across, according to the number to be served. Roll them in the dried crumbs, then in beaten egg, then again in the crumbs.

Heat enough olive oil in a wide, shallow saucepan to come 2.5 cm (1 in) deep, until the surface begins to tremble. Put in the croquettes. Use a slotted spoon to turn them and cook for about 4 minutes, until golden on the outside. Remove onto paper to drain – in Greece this would be newspaper.

In a flameproof casserole, combine the vinegar, wine, honey, 4-5 tablespoons breadcrumbs and 50 g (2 oz) chopped walnuts. Season with salt and pepper and bring to the boil. Add the croquettes and simmer for about 10 minutes. Add the parsley, shake the pan to make sure the croquettes aren't sticking and simmer for another 2-5 minutes. Serve warm or cold, garnished with the remaining walnuts.

ASTAKÓS PLAKÍ

LOBSTER IN TOMATO SAUCE WITH SAFFRON RICE

Lobsters in Greece are the spiny lobsters of the Mediterranean or the Pacific, not the large clawed homard of the Atlantic. This dish is delicious with either, provided they are alive or only recently killed when you buy them. Crab can also be substituted. Serve it with the saffron rice, some crusty bread and a cucumber salad, with fresh fruit for dessert.

SERVES 4-6

2 live or recently dead lobsters, about 800 g-1 kg
(1¾-2 lb) each
25 strands saffron, soaked in 50 ml (2 fl oz)
hot water
100 g (4 oz) onion, finely chopped
1 medium-sized leek, washed and finely chopped
7-9 tablespoons fruity olive oil
3 garlic cloves, finely chopped
500 g (1 lb) tomatoes, skinned, seeded and the flesh
finely chopped
3-4 sun-dried tomatoes (in oil, page 16, or soaked
in 125 ml [4 fl oz] boiling water), pounded to a paste,
or 2 teaspoons tomato purée, with the water
125 ml (4 fl oz) white wine
50 ml (2 fl oz) orange juice
1 bay leaf
salt and freshly ground pepper
25 g (1 oz) fresh fennel, finely chopped
25 g (1 oz) flat leaf parsley, finely chopped
1 tablespoon fresh mint, finely chopped
Saffron rice (see page 91) to serve

If you have live lobsters, plunge them into a pan of boiling water for 1 minute, then into cold water.

To prepare the lobsters, break off the claws and crack them open with a hammer. Cut off the tip of the tail (with the fins), then sever the tail where it joins the head with a heavy knife. Cut the tail into rings, slicing through the shell between the ribs.

Split the head open lengthways with a hard blow of a knife and remove and discard the gritty stomach sac. Put the coral (if any) and the green matter (which is the liver) into a sieve over a bowl, sprinkle with salt

RED MULLET FOR SALE *The barboúnia, or red mullet, has long been highly prized by the Greeks.*

and pepper and reserve. Put the saffron to soak.

In a heavy-bottomed pan big enough to contain the lobsters and sauce, fry the onion and leek gently in 3 tablespoons olive oil until transparent. Add the garlic, chopped tomatoes, tomato soaking liquid and purée (or tomato paste), wine, orange juice and bay leaf. Season and simmer, covered, for 15 minutes.

Add the fennel, parsley, mint, saffron and liquid and lobster tail pieces and claws with their shells (but not the legs) and simmer, covered, for 10 minutes.

In the meantime push the coral and liver of the lobster through the sieve and beat the purée with 4-6 tablespoons olive oil. When the lobster has simmered 10 minutes, ladle out about 200 ml (7 fl oz) sauce and beat this into the coral purée. Pour this back into the pot, stir and simmer for another 10 minutes. Serve with saffron rice.

KRÓKOS PILÁFI

SAFFRON RICE

This golden, beautifully perfumed rice is a simple, elegant accompaniment to most dishes. Leave it plain to serve with lobster. At other times you might want to sprinkle it with fresh herbs or mist it with rosewater.

SERVES 4

25 saffron strands
250 g (8 oz) Basmati rice
2 tablespoons olive oil
salt to taste

Soak the saffron in 125 ml (4 fl oz) hot water for 10-15 minutes. Put the rice in a sieve and rinse under hot water until it runs clear. Then rinse again under cold water and leave to drain.

Heat the oil in a saucepan and add the rice. Sauté until it becomes translucent. Add 600 ml (1 pt) water and salt, bring to the boil and add the saffron infusion. Stir, cover tightly and leave to simmer on a very low heat (preferably on a heat diffuser) – for about 20 minutes, until craters form on the surface.

Stretch a piece of muslin or a tea towel over the top, cover tightly with a lid and leave in a warm corner, to rest for 10-15 minutes. The cloth will absorb the steam from the rice and allow the grains to separate.

ASTAKÓS PLAKÍ *left (p. 89)*, KRÓKOS PILÁFI *right*

CHTAPÓTHI KRASSÁTO

OCTOPUS IN WINE

My friend Paul comes to the island every year. And every year he takes his mask and snorkel to the same deserted spot to visit an old friend – a venerable octopus who comes out from the recesses of the sunken rocks to greet him. They play draughts together. Paul doesn't like this recipe, but most Greeks love it.

Some people cook potatoes, rice or pasta in the pot with the octopus. I prefer them cooked separately. This is a rich dish, and it doesn't really matter if the octopus has expelled all its ink while being caught. Just omit the ink from the recipe. The stew doesn't need more than a nice mixed salad and perhaps a granita for dessert.

SERVES 4

1 kg (2 lb) octopus
50 ml (2 fl oz) olive oil
250 g (8 oz) onions, finely chopped
350 g (12 oz) tomatoes, skinned, seeded and the flesh finely chopped
2 sun-dried tomatoes (if in oil see page 16), snipped up and soaked in 50 ml (2 fl oz) boiling water, or 1 teaspoon tomato paste
250 ml (8 fl oz) mavrotháphne *(see page 17), or ruby port*
1 teaspoon scorthostoúmbi, *garlic vinegar (see page 25) or wine vinegar*
2 celery stalks or celery tops and leaves, finely chopped
1 bay leaf, crushed
salt and freshly ground black pepper

To clean the octopus, stretch out the tentacles all in one direction and slash across, above and below the eyes to remove them. Pop out the beak in the middle of the mouth. Pull out the entrails from inside the head, saving the ink sac, which looks very silvery. Turn the octopus body inside out and wash inside. Don't worry about the skin, but run your hands down the tentacles and pop out any big suckers.

Put the ink sac (if it is there) in a sieve placed over a cup. Crush the ink sac with the back of a wooden spoon. Pour a tablespoon of water through and crush again, extracting as much ink as possible. Put the ink in the refrigerator until needed.

The fishermen in Greece beat the octopus against the rocks 80 times before they sell it. In case your octopus hasn't been given the same treatment, you might whack it a bit with a meat cleaver or rolling pin. Cut it into bite-sized pieces.

Place the octopus pieces in a dry pot, set on a heat diffuser over the lowest possible heat, and sweat until it exudes then reabsorbs its own red liquid, or until

tender. This could take anywhere from 20-30 minutes.

Remove the octopus and any remaining liquid, add the olive oil and fry the onions gently until transparent. Pound the sun-dried tomatoes to a paste, then add the chopped tomato, tomato paste, *mavrotháphne*, garlic or wine vinegar, celery and bay leaf to the pan, and season with salt and pepper. Simmer 5-10 minutes until the sauce begins to thicken.

Add the octopus, cover and simmer slowly for about 50 minutes. Stir in the ink (if reserved) and simmer another 10 minutes, or until tender.

PALAMÍTHA I XYFÍAS TOURSÍ

PICKLED BONITO OR SWORDFISH WITH GREEN TOMATOES

If you grow your own tomatoes or come from the American south or parts of Italy, then you probably know and love the green tomato for itself. They should be smoothly sour, crunchy and green, green, green. If your greengrocer doesn't sell them, try Mexican *tomatillos*, or – if you must – unripe 'ripe' tomatoes, which will make a slightly different dish.

This dish of marinated raw fish is wonderful as a hors d'œuvre, a first course, or as part of a buffet. Bonito is a nice light-coloured tuna, with less dense flesh than the better-known tuna. Swordfish, with its rings of flesh, is very similar.

SERVES 6-8

1.2 kg (2½ lb) very fresh bonito or swordfish, cut into 2 cm (¾ in) cubes or scallops
250 g (8 oz) onions, thinly sliced
3-4 tablespoons olive oil
500 g (1 lb) green tomatoes, roughly chopped
1-2 small hot red fresh chillies, or ¼-½ teaspoon cayenne pepper (according to taste)
2 garlic cloves, sliced
15 g (½ oz) fresh mint, chopped
salt
250 ml (8 fl oz) fresh lemon juice (5-8 lemons)

In a heavy frying-pan, fry the onions gently in the olive oil until barely transparent. Add the tomatoes, chillies, garlic, mint and some salt. Stir over high heat for 1-2 minutes. Remove the sauce and cool.

In a wide dish layer the raw fish with the tomato mixture and pour in the lemon juice to cover everything. Cover lightly and leave this to macerate in the refrigerator for 24-36 hours.

DRYING OCTOPUS *Air-dried octopus is kept in preparation for fast days, when no fish with blood may be eaten.*

BAKALIÁROS CAPODÍSTRIAS

SALT COD AND POTATO GRATIN WITH GARLIC AND HERBS

This is a straightforward, earthy dish with political undertones. Capodistrias, who was the first head of Greece's provisional government during its struggle for independence from the Ottoman Empire, spent a few years of exile in Geneva, where he was introduced to the potato. On his journey home, he brought samples of this nutritious new food with him. The Greeks refused to share his enthusiasm until he had some potato cuttings planted in the public gardens, surrounded by a fence and posted with a sentry. He proclaimed the potato forbidden to the public, making them instantly irresistible. Stolen cuttings were planted surreptitiously all around the country . . .

Serve this gratin with a huge mixed salad.

SERVES 6

1.2-1.4 kg (2¾-3 lb) side of salt cod
4 waxy potatoes, about 250 g (8 oz) each
4 tablespoons olive oil
6 garlic cloves, finely chopped
50 g (2 oz) flat leaf parsley, finely chopped
25 g (1 oz) fresh dill, finely chopped
20 saffron strands, soaked in 2 tablespoons boiling water
350 g (12 oz) thick Greek yogurt
40 g (1½ oz) paximáthia, bread rusks (see page 10) or stale wholemeal breadcrumbs
salt

TO SIMMER THE FISH

1 medium-sized onion, stuck with a clove
1 small leek, washed
100 g (4 oz) carrots, scraped
tops and leaves of 1 celery stalk, roughly chopped
2 garlic cloves
2 bay leaves
2 sprigs of flat leaf parsley
10 black peppercorns
1 lemon, quartered
2 lemon or scented geranium leaves (optional)

Rinse all the loose salt off the *bakaliáros*, salt cod side, then soak for 24 hours. Some people put it in a large bowl under running water, but I prefer an even larger bucket, as you can cover the dried fish well with a greater amount of water to dissolve the salt and plump up the flesh. Change the water 3-4 times during the 24 hours.

Place the simmering ingredients in a large soup pot. Scrub but do not peel the potatoes. Add them to the pot and cover generously with water – enough to cover the salt cod when it is added. Bring this to the boil and simmer for 15 minutes. Add the salt cod, cut into chunks, and simmer 10-15 minutes – until the fish is firm and tender.

Remove the fish to a platter or board. Check the potatoes, which should also be tender but firm. When they are done, remove and refresh them under cold running water.

Strain the broth through a fine sieve (or a colander lined with cheesecloth or muslin), pressing on the vegetables with the back of a wooden spoon. Reserve about 125 ml (4 fl oz) broth – perhaps a little more – for this dish: the rest can be used as soup stock.

When the fish is cool enough to handle, remove all the skin and bones and discard them, along with any bits of fish that are not succulent and tender. (Here you need a cat.) The remaining fish should break into medallions and slivers almost on its own. Put it into an oiled baking dish or earthenware casserole large enough to hold the fish and potatoes.

Peel and slice the potatoes. Toss them gently with the fish, 3 tablespoons olive oil, garlic, parsley and dill. Taste and adjust for salt.

Beat together the yogurt with the soaked saffron strands and their liquid and the reserved fish stock. Pour over the fish and potatoes (adding a little more stock if needed). Sauté the breadcrumbs in 1 tablespoon oil until golden, then sprinkle over the top. Bake in an oven preheated to 180°C (350°F, gas 4) for about 30 minutes.

SAVÓRO

PICKLED FISH

Savóro or pickled fish is something one finds anywhere around the Mediterranean where there are fishermen. It is natural that they should pickle whatever they cannot eat or sell of the day's catch. In Hydra they fry large batches of fish, eat what they can and pickle the rest. I have made this version with baked, rather than fried fish, as it is a bit healthier.

WAVES OF PINK *Fishing nets create the effect of waves rippling in the breeze.*

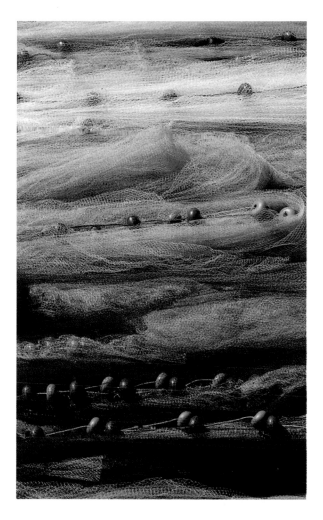

I very often make kilos of this, serve it hot without the vinegar and oil, and pickle the rest for later. It is wonderful served as a luncheon or first course. I also like it as an accompaniment to soup.

SERVES 8

1 kg fish (2 lb) sardines, small mackerel, needle fish (gar) or your choice
250 g (8 oz) mild Spanish onions, finely chopped
3 tablespoons fruity olive oil
300 g (10 oz) tomatoes, skinned, seeded and flesh chopped
4-6 garlic cloves
tops and leaves of 4-6 celery stalks, finely chopped
1 tablespoon mountain thyme (see page 16)
2 teaspoons fresh rosemary
1 small dried red chilli, whole
1 bay leaf
salt and freshly ground black pepper
125 ml (4 fl oz) white wine

DRESSING
25 g (1 oz) flat leaf parsley, finely chopped
125 ml (4 fl oz) good wine vinegar
125 ml (4 fl oz) fruity olive oil

If you are using sardines or mackerel, clean and gut them normally. If you are using needle fish, break off the heads just under the gills without severing the innards. Then carefully pull the head away, removing the innards at the same time. Rinse all the fish carefully and lay them side by side in a glass or earthenware baking dish.

In a medium-sized heavy frying-pan, fry the onions gently in the olive oil until transparent. Add the chopped tomatoes, garlic, celery, thyme, rosemary, chilli and bay leaf, with salt and pepper and the wine. Simmer for 10 minutes then pour over the fish.

Put the dish in an oven preheated to 180°C (350°F, gas 4) on the middle shelf, and bake for 10-15 minutes, until the fish is just cooked. Sprinkle with parsley, pour in the vinegar and cover with a light film of olive oil. Cool and refrigerate for 24-36 hours before serving. Provided the fish are completely covered by the vinegar and oil, they will keep safely for 5 days.

HÉLI SPETZIÓTIKO

EEL SPETZES-STYLE WITH TOMATO SAUCE AND FETA

Eel is not easy to find these days but well worth looking for. The Spetzioti are said to keep them in their water cisterns, but this is not why the dish is called 'Spetziótiko'. These islanders have lent their name to any dish that is baked in tomato sauce with *féta*, and in fact this method can be used for many other fish.

Get your fishmonger to clean the eel for you. If you want to do it yourself, however, make a slit all the way round, just under the head. Turn the skin back, so that you can grip it. This is easier with salty fingers. Hold the head with a kitchen towel and peel the skin back, all the way and off. (If there is brown fat under the skin take this off too.) Clean the eel by making an incision up the belly, and cut off the head then wash the cavity.

SERVES 4-5

1 kg (2 lb) moray, conger or freshwater eel, skinned, gutted and washed, head removed and cut into 8 cm (2½ in) pieces
2-3 tablespoons olive oil
250 g (8 oz) onions, roughly chopped
3-4 sun-dried tomatoes (in oil, see page 16), or snipped up and soaked in 2-3 tablespoons boiling water, or 1 tablespoon tomato paste
350 g (12 oz) tomatoes, skinned, seeded and the flesh chopped
½ teaspoon honey
1 tablespoon fresh thyme or ½ teaspoon mountain thyme (see page 16)
1 bay leaf, crumbled
finely grated zest of 1 lemon, with 1 teaspoon juice
2-3 garlic cloves, finely chopped
50 g (2 oz) flat leaf parsley, finely chopped
1 tablespoon fresh mint, finely chopped
salt and freshly ground black pepper
250 g (8 oz) féta cheese, crumbled

In a heavy frying-pan or wide flameproof casserole heat 2 tablespoons olive oil and sauté the eel pieces until well-browned on all sides. Remove from the pan and add another tablespoon oil if necessary.

Add the onions and fry gently until translucent. Pound the sun-dried tomatoes, if using, to a paste. Then add the chopped tomatoes, tomato paste, honey, thyme, bay leaf, lemon zest and garlic to the pan and simmer for 10-12 minutes until the sauce begins to thicken.

Return the eel pieces to the sauce and stir in the parsley and mint, seasoning with salt and pepper. Move to a baking dish or earthenware casserole, if necessary. Strew with the crumbled *féta* and shake the dish, so the cheese settles a little. Sprinkle with lemon juice. Bake in an oven preheated to 180°C (350°F, gas 4) for about 30 minutes.

SFYRÍTHA ME LAHANIKÁ

GROUPER STEAMED WITH CHOPPED VEGETABLES

There is nothing better than a big steamed fish, veiled in vegetables. If you like, you can make egg and lemon sauce (*see page 104*) with the stock and pour it over the fish. Or pass a bowl of *latholémono*, the lemon-olive dressing (*see page 86*).

SERVES 6

3.6 kg (8 lb) whole grouper, sea bass, red snapper or fresh cod, scaled and gutted, gills removed (see page 85)
3-4 tablespoons fruity olive oil
100 g (4 oz) onion, finely chopped
1 medium-sized leek, washed and thinly sliced, including the light green
250 g (8 oz) carrots, finely diced
250 g (8 oz) turnips, peeled and finely diced
200 g (7 oz) courgettes, washed and finely diced
3 celery stalks, finely chopped
1 bay leaf, crushed
400 g (1½ oz) parsley stems
1 tablespoon thyme or 1 teaspoon mountain thyme (see page 16)

*1 teaspoon oregano or ¼ teaspoon mountain
oregano* (see page 15)
salt and freshly ground black pepper
250 ml (8 fl oz) dry white wine
*2 strips thinly pared lemon zest,
about 5 cm (2 in) long*
1 teaspoon lemon juice
2 lemons, cut into wedges, to garnish
avgolémono, egg and lemon sauce
(see page 104 – optional)

In a heavy-bottomed saucepan heat the olive oil, then
add all the vegetables and herbs and season with salt
and pepper. Toss over high heat for 1-2 minutes. Pour
in the wine, 450 ml (16 fl oz) water and add the
lemon zest and juice. Bring to the boil and simmer for
2 minutes.

If the fish is too long to fit any roasting pan or
poacher you have, you may have (sadly) to remove the
head, or cut the fish in half. Line the bottom of a large
fish kettle or roasting tin with double-strength foil, or
a piece of cheesecloth or muslin, to enable you to lift
the fish out easily when it is done.

Wash the fish inside, pat dry and season it. Arrange
it on the foil and pour the hot vegetables and their
liquid round it. Bake in an oven preheated to 180°C
(350°F, gas 4) for 45-60 minutes, until the flesh is
opaque and firm, but still juicy.

Remove the pan from the oven, scrape the
vegetables off the surface of the fish and, holding each
end of the foil or cheesecloth, lift it out. Slide it onto
a warmed platter (arranging the pieces back in the
original shape, if it was cut). Remove the skin and
fins carefully, and scrape off any brown flesh.

Smother with vegetables, lifting them from the
stock with a slotted spoon. Serve garnished with
lemon wedges.

MÍTHIA YEMISTÁ

STUFFED MUSSELS

This is a Lenten dish which is enjoyed whenever
mussels are in season.

SERVES 4-6

1.1 kg (2½ lb) live mussels
125 ml (4 fl oz) white wine
salt and freshly ground black pepper
700 ml (1¼ fl oz) fish stock or herb broth
(see page 37)
350 g (12 oz) onions, finely chopped
4 tablespoons olive oil
100 g (4 oz) Basmati rice, washed (see page 91)
65 g (2½ oz) pine nuts
65 g (2½ oz) currants
1 tablespoon finely chopped flat leaf parsley
1 tablespoon finely chopped fresh dill
2 tablespoons finely chopped fresh mint
*handfuls of fresh lemon leaves, or vine or
lettuce leaves plus a strip of lemon zest*
2-3 lemons, cut into wedges, to garnish

Scrub the mussels under running water, discarding any
that are not closed. In a large pan bring the stock to the
boil with the wine, season, and put in the mussels.
Cover and simmer until the shells open. Remove from
the pan and discard any that remain closed. Clean
away the beards, refresh them by dropping them into a
bowl of cold water, then drain and reserve.

In a heavy frying-pan fry the onions gently in the
olive oil until translucent. Add the washed rice and
sauté until transparent. Add 50 ml (2 fl oz) mussel
stock, cover and simmer for about 15 minutes – until
all the liquid has been absorbed. Gently stir in the
pine nuts, currants, parsley, dill and mint. Taste and
season with salt and pepper and leave to cool.

Fill each mussel shell with some of the stuffing.
Close the shells again tightly and tie with thread. Line
a saucepan which will take the mussels in 2-3 layers
with lemon leaves. Pack in the mussels and pour the
remaining mussel stock over them. Simmer for
20-30 minutes. Then drain off any remaining liquid.
Serve hot or cold, garnished with lemon wedges.

MEAT, POULTRY AND GAME

Special occasions and festive gatherings call for prized lamb, beef and pork dishes, while poultry and game form the basis of classic family fare.

HIRINÓ ME KYTHÓNIA (*p. 111*)

Arapogiannis, Black John, arrives at the building site with a crowing, kicking basket in tow. Vasilis, his family, a few close friends and the local *papás*, priest, are already there. Arapogiannis, massive and strong, pulls a magnificent cock from the basket. He smooths his ebony-emerald breast and looks him in the eye while whispering endearments to calm his feathered fury. With one strong, swift movement, the cock's head flies off and Arapogiannis holds the bleeding corpse over the earth. The priest then chants a blessing while pouring holy wine over the same spot. Vasilis tosses in a coin and Arapogiannis lays the first foundation stone for Vasilis' new house. The significance of shelter in Greek life is primitively expressed in this ancient ritual. The entire company returns to Kiria Sophia's house to celebrate this solemn, happy occasion with an island feast.

Kiria Sophia, who came to the island as a bride between the world wars, used to have her own tavern. Now in semi-retirement, she cooks privately. She is a lovable old crony with flashing black eyes and golden teeth who needs cajoling to cook. Once your flattery hits the mark, she imperiously starts a litany of provisions you must buy and carry up the hill to her. The bargain is struck. She will make an assortment of *mezethákia*, a *tyrópitta*, cheese pie, the fresh *féta* coming from her grandson who is a shepherd, *kotópoulo me bámies kokkinistó*, chicken and okra in tomato sauce, with *kritharáki* or *sousamáki*, little pastas that look like barley or sesame. She has *kokinélli*, a light resinated rose wine that her son made . . . and whatever fruit you decide to provide for dessert.

Kiria Sophia cooks this meal in a kitchen that hasn't changed in 200 years. She is as adept at controlling her fires as we would be with our gas and electric ranges. This day, she grabs Vasilis' daughters, presents her rosy cheeks to be kissed and tells them to take the *mezéthes* to the table. She shoves some jugs at Vasilis, ordering him to fill them from one of the barrels in the *trapezaría*, or dining room, which is like the inside of a rainbow. The wooden ceiling is painted pink, green and lavender and is hung with muslin bags full of flour, grains and pulses. The entire room is illuminated by Kiria Sophia's sense of colour and all the past feasts celebrated there. When this happy meal is almost over, she shuffles in from the kitchen, empty glass in hand. She pulls up a pink chair next to Vasilis, bangs her glass down for him to fill and toasts her own good health, *hygia mas*.

Meat, game and poultry have always been reserved for special occasions in Greece. The fast or feast days of the church harmonize well with the sparse landscape which cannot produce endless edible beasts. In fact, a friend Iris claims that her grandfather 'ate three houses in Omonia', the Athenian equivalent of Piccadilly Circus, by demanding meat twice a day along with his soup. In modest island homes, all the recipes in this chapter would be served on Sundays or feast days.

Turkeys are stuffed with ground lamb and pine nuts at Christmas. Most of Greece is outdoors from early morning on Easter Sunday tending whole baby lambs, which they take turns at turning on the *soúvla*, spit. Suckling pig on the spit would be an appropriate meal to celebrate a marriage or christening. Most of the islands lie in the migration pattern of many prized game birds, and the islanders look forward to the hunting season and its rewards. It is common among islanders to cook game in tomato sauce, which I haven't often come across elsewhere.

Offal is not much mentioned in this book, but esteemed in Greece nevertheless. Lamb or kid brains, kidney and testicles are considered delicacies. *Piktí* is jellied veal or pig's head flavoured with bitter orange. One must be on best terms with the butcher to get lamb or kid liver, which is best with least preparation – lightly grilled or sautéed with a squeeze of lemon is the traditional way. *Loukánika* are spicy, pork sausages which have been made the same way since ancient times and *garthoúmbes* are delicious sausages made from lamb or kid.

ARNÁKI FRIKASSÉ

FRICASSEE OF SPRING LAMB WITH COS LETTUCE

Cos lettuce, otherwise known as romaine, originated on the island of Cos. Hippocrates recommended that it be eaten at the end of a meal for its sleep-inducing effect. Indeed, the latex of wild lettuce does contain traces of soporific elements. *Arnáki frikassé*, a favourite Greek dish, was not devised as a national sedative, however.

It is made with young spring lamb, still milk-fed at this time of the year, or with kid. Some people blanch the lettuce for 2-3 minutes, to reduce the bitterness, before they add it. I value the bitter note it contributes. The final touch is made with orange flower water. I use an atomizer to spray the dish. I don't want you to taste the orange flower water, but to feel as though you walked through an orange grove on the way to the dinner table.

You might find it easier to buy the lamb cubed, or to buy 6-8 shoulder chops, one for each person.

SERVES 6-8

1.1-1.4 kg (2½-3 lb) boned spring lamb, from the leg or shoulder

100 g (4 oz) onion, finely chopped

3 tablespoons olive oil

grated zest of 1 lemon

1 teaspoon honey

salt and freshly ground black pepper

about 600 ml (1 pt) herb broth (see page 37) or water

TO FINISH

2 large heads Cos lettuce, about 1 kg (2 lb), washed and shredded

2 bunches spring onions, cleaned and chopped, including the greens

50 g (2 oz) fresh dill, chopped

15 g (½ oz) fresh mint, chopped

2 teaspoons olive oil

grated zest of 1 lemon and juice of 2 lemons

1 teaspoon flour

2 medium-sized eggs

¼ teaspoon orange flower water

Remove the skin and excess fat from the lamb and cut into pieces, each being the size of one portion.

In a large pot big enough to take everything, fry the onion gently in the olive oil until transparent. Add the lamb and turn until well browned on all sides. Stir in the grated lemon zest and the honey and season the meat with salt and pepper. Barely cover with water or herb broth and simmer for 45 minutes. (You can cook ahead up to this point.)

Add the shredded lettuce, spring onions, dill and mint and continue simmering for about 30 minutes, until the meat is tender. (It may take a bit longer if you don't have real milk-fed spring lamb or kid.) There should be 450-600 ml (16-20 fl oz) of liquid in the pot.

In a cup, beat 2 teaspoons olive oil with the finely grated zest of the second lemon and the juice of both. Put the flour in a small saucepan, stirring in enough lemon/oil to make a smooth paste. Gradually stir in the rest of the lemon/oil until it is emulsified. Put the saucepan over low heat and slowly add 250 ml (8 fl oz) stock from the pot. Stir and cook for about 5 minutes.

Beat the eggs in a bowl. Slowly pour in the hot lemon/oil mixture, beating all the while. Return to a very low heat and add as much as possible of the stock remaining in the pot. Stir for about 5 minutes.

Pour the sauce back over the lamb and stir or shake the pan to incorporate the egg/lemon sauce into the fricassee. Remove to a well-warmed platter and sprinkle with orange flower water.

CRETAN OLIVE GROVES (*overleaf*)

LÁHANO YEMISTÓ

STUFFED CABBAGE WITH EGG AND LEMON SAUCE

This is a dramatic-looking version of an old Balkan and Middle Eastern stand-by – stuffed cabbage. The recipe may look long but it is in fact not at all difficult. Surround the cabbage cake with steamed vegetables such as carrots and small whole onions, or with courgettes and leeks. Accompany it with a tomato salad and crusty bread. Try the *zvíngi*, fritters with honey syrup, on page 134 for dessert.

If the minced meat is fattier than you like, the following method of boiling it first is tried and true in this part of the world. It is not a *nouvelle* innovation. It can also provide the stock for the recipe.

SERVES 6-8

1 whole cabbage, about 1.3 kg (3 lb)
1 kg (2 lb) minced lamb (or beef or pork)
500 g (1 lb) Basmati or long-grain rice, rinsed and soaked (see page 91)
4 tablespoons fruity olive oil
¼ teaspoon freshly ground cinnamon
⅛ teaspoon freshly ground clove
salt
1 teaspoon freshly ground black pepper
350 ml (12 fl oz) stock (from the pot if rendering the meat) or water
75 g (3 oz) pine nuts
100 g (4 oz) currants
1 big bunch spring onions, white and light green chopped
40 g (1½ oz) flat leaf parsley, chopped
25 g (1 oz) fresh dill, chopped
1 tablespoon chopped fresh mint

TO COOK THE CABBAGE CAKE

1 tablespoon olive oil
2 tablespoons oúzo
50 ml (2 fl oz) stock (from the pot if rendering the meat) or water
2 bay leaves
2 sprigs thyme
4-5 lemon, cabbage or scented geranium leaves
1 sprig of fresh mint

EGG AND LEMON SAUCE AND GARNISH

3 medium-sized eggs, separated
grated zest of 1 lemon, juice of 3
1 teaspoon cornflour
350 ml (12 fl oz) stock (from the pot if you are rendering the meat) or herb broth (see page 37)
1 tablespoon finely chopped parsley
1 tablespoon finely chopped dill
¼ teaspoon mint, finely chopped

If rendering the minced meat, bring a stock pot, with about 3 litres (5 pt) of water, to a rolling boil and immediately turn it down to a simmer. Sprinkle in the minced meat, rubbing it between your fingers into tiny pieces. Simmer for about 10 minutes, rendering most of the fat. Skim off the fat and drain the meat in a sieve, reserving the broth.

Return the broth to the pot (or use water), bring it to the boil, then turn the heat off. Submerge the whole cabbage in the liquid, weight it with a plate, and leave for 1 hour.

In a large heavy frying-pan, sauté the minced lamb in 3 tablespoons olive oil until well browned. Add the rinsed rice, cinnamon, clove, salt and pepper and continue sautéing until the rice is transparent.

Take 350 ml (12 fl oz) stock from the cabbage pot and add it, 50 ml (2 fl oz) at a time, to the frying-pan, until it has all been absorbed and the rice is *al dente*. Add the pine nuts, currants, spring onions, parsley, dill and mint, and adjust the salt.

Remove the cabbage from the broth and detach the leaves. Choose a bowl that will fit inside the stock pot. It must be large enough to hold all the stuffing with room to spare for the cabbage. Oil the inside lightly and line it with a double layer of cabbage leaves, arranging the outside leaves in a pleasing pattern. Fill half-way with stuffing. Cover with a layer of cabbage. Fill with the remaining stuffing and cover with a final layer of cabbage.

Pour 1 tablespoon of oil, the *oúzo* and 50 ml (2 fl oz) of stock over the cabbage. Weight the top with a plate. Put another upside-down plate (or a trivet) in the stock pot and put in the bowl. The stock should come half way up the sides of the bowl. Strew bay leaves, thyme, lemon or other leaves and mint into the stock round the bowl. Cover the pot tightly, bring to a simmer and steam for 1¼ hours.

When the cabbage cake is done, make the sauce. In a saucepan or the top of a double boiler beat the egg yolk with the lemon zest and juice and the cornflour. Over low heat, slowly add 350 ml (12 floz) hot stock by the spoonful, and continue cooking over low heat, until you have a rich sauce.

Whisk the egg whites in a separate bowl until soft peaks form. Fold these into the sauce and stir until hot.

To serve, place a warmed platter over the bowl of

INQUISITIVE CREATURES *A herd of goats admire the view from the top of an ancient water cistern on Hydra.*

cabbage cake. Reverse them and lift off the bowl. Top with a few spoonfuls of egg and lemon sauce and sprinkle with fresh herbs. Surround the cake with steamed vegetables and serve with the rest of the sauce in a boat.

PAÏTHÁKIA TIS SKÁRAS

SPICY LAMB CHOPS

The marinade in this recipe is good for spicing up any grilled meat or poultry without completely overpowering it. In Greece, the chops would weigh much less than 75 g (3 oz), as the lamb is slaughtered much younger and you would need many more than two per person.

SERVES 6

*12 loin lamb chops, about 75 g (3 oz) each,
trimmed of excess fat
1 hot dried red chilli, soaked in boiling water for
1 hour, or ¼ teaspoon cayenne
finely grated zest and 2 tablespoons juice from
1 lemon
1 garlic clove, finely chopped
¼ teaspoon freshly ground coriander seed
¼ teaspoon salt
1 tablespoon grated onion
2 teaspoons honey
2 tablespoons spicy olive oil*

Remove the seeds from the soaked red chilli if you don't like things too hot and put it in a mortar with the grated zest, garlic, coriander and salt. Pound with a pestle to a smooth paste, adding a few drops of lemon juice to moisten if necessary. Pound in the onion and beat with the lemon juice, honey and olive oil to make a thick, smooth emulsion. Coat each lamb chop with the spicy emulsion and leave to marinate for 2 hours.

Wipe the chops and put under a hot grill – or grill them over hot embers (if you have grape vine cuttings or juniper wood all the better). Grill them for about 4 minutes on each side if they are small and you like them very rare – a couple of minutes longer if you prefer them less pink – brushing with a thin coat of marinade when you turn them. Serve with extra slices of lemon and perhaps the vegetable pilaf on page 57.

KLÉFTIKO

LAMB, CHEESE AND TOMATOES IN FILO PACKETS

This dish is named after the guerillas of the Greek War of Independence who bear the same name. It is said that they cooked their food over fires in packets like these, so they could grab their meal and run in one movement if the need arose. Those were not the most appetizing circumstances in which to enjoy a formidable dish.

The recipe makes 6 main course packets. You could make 8 smaller ones to serve as appetizers by using extra filo sheets.

SERVES 6

*1 kg (2 lb) boned lamb, from the leg or shoulder,
in 2.5 cm (1 in) cubes
250 g (8 oz) onions, sliced
2 tablespoons fruity olive oil
½ teaspoon crushed rosemary
300 g (10 oz) tomatoes, skinned, seeded and the
flesh chopped
salt and freshly ground pepper
250 g (9 oz) féta cheese
2 garlic cloves, finely chopped
25 g (1 oz) flat leaf parsley, finely chopped*
PASTRY PARCEL
*12 sheets of filo pastry, 50 x 30 cm (20 x 12 in),
defrosted
about 125 ml (4 fl oz) olive oil
1½-2 teaspoons cracked wheat (bulgar) or rice
1 tablespoon sesame seeds*

In a large flameproof casserole, heat the oil in 2 tablespoons olive oil. Fry the onions over gentle heat until transparent. Add the cubed lamb and brown on all sides. Add the rosemary and chopped tomatoes and season with salt and pepper. Simmer for 15-20 minutes (depending on the cut – 15 minutes for the shoulder, 25 for the leg). The sauce should be reduced and quite thick.

Crumble the *féta* with the garlic and chopped parsley and reserve. Unwrap the filo and place under a damp cloth, removing only one sheet at a time. Place one sheet on a work surface and brush it evenly with olive oil. Place a second layer directly on top and brush with a layer of olive oil. Sprinkle a pinch (¼ teaspoon or less) of rice or cracked wheat over the middle of the pastry, leaving a 7.5 cm (3 in) border on all sides.

Roughly divide the meat by the number of packets you wish to make – 6 or 8. Spoon a portion of meat and sauce over the central area, and sprinkle with a little of the crumbled *féta* mixture. Fold the filo ends over the filling, then fold the sides inward. Roll it up, making sure the sides stay tucked in. Place the envelope, seam-side down, on an oiled or non-stick baking sheet. Brush the top with olive oil and sprinkle with sesame seeds. Continue until you have used up all the filling.

Bake in an oven preheated to 180°C (350°F, gas 4) for about 30 minutes until the filo packets are golden brown.

MOSHARÁKI MELITZÁNES

VEAL OR BEEF STEW
WITH AUBERGINE

In Homeric days, when wealth was measured in cattle, the slaughter and serving of a bull to a guest was the highest sign of honour. As the Greek landscape has never been well suited to pasturage, this dish of veal or young beef with aubergine would still provide a festival or Sunday meal.

I used small banana-shaped aubergines for this. If you don't like aubergines, these can be replaced by okra. Be sure to prepare this first (*see page 23*) to remove the mucous.

SERVES 6-8

1 kg (2 lb) aubergines, cubed
salt and freshly ground black pepper
4-5 tablespoons olive oil
375-400 g (13·14 oz) onions, chopped
1 kg (2 lb) pink veal or braising beef, cut into
5 cm (2 in) cubes
2 teaspoons freshly ground coriander seed
½ teaspoon freshly ground cinnamon
¼ teaspoon freshly ground allspice
1 teaspoon paprika
¼-½ teaspoon cayenne pepper
4 garlic cloves, finely chopped
2 bay leaves
1 kg (2 lb) tomatoes, skinned, seeded and the
flesh chopped, or slightly less, plus 1 teaspoon
tomato paste or 2 sun-dried tomatoes, snipped up,
soaked in 125 ml (4 fl oz) water and pounded
400-450 ml (14-16 fl oz) red wine or water
juice of 1-2 lemons, to taste
40 g (1½ oz) flat leaf parsley, chopped

Soak the aubergine cubes in a bowl of heavily salted water for 30 minutes. Drain and rinse them, then dry well.

In a heavy-bottomed pot, big enough to hold everything, heat 3-4 tablespoons olive oil and sauté the aubergine cubes until brown. Remove the aubergines and reserve them, adding 1 tablespoon olive oil and the onions to the pot. Fry over gentle heat until transparent.

Add the meat cubes and sauté until they are brown on all sides. Sprinkle with the ground coriander, cinnamon, allspice, paprika, cayenne and garlic and add the bay leaves, seasoning with salt and pepper. Fry, stirring constantly, for 1-2 minutes.

Add the chopped tomato and tomato paste, stir and simmer for 10 minutes. Add most of the wine or water to cover, and simmer slowly, over low heat, until the meat is tender – 1½-2 hours – adding wine or water as needed.

When the meat is tender, but not falling apart, stir in the aubergine cubes and simmer for 20 minutes. Add the lemon juice to taste and parsley and simmer for a further 10 minutes.

Serve with steamed rice, cracked wheat (*see page 120*) or barley flakes.

PSITÓ ME PILÁFI-VÍSINO

ROAST MARINATED FILLET OF BEEF WITH CHERRY PILAF

This Sunday dinner with a fruity blush is best served with a salad of wild greens.

SERVES 6

1 kg (2 lb) fillet of beef, trimmed and tied
125 ml (4 fl oz) cherry brandy
125 ml (4 fl oz) red wine
1-2 garlic cloves, finely chopped
2 bay leaves, crushed
1 teaspoon mountain thyme (see page 16)
10 black peppercorns, lightly crushed
1 teaspoon coriander seeds, lightly crushed
2 teaspoons olive oil
¼ teaspoon salt
pilάfi-visinό, cherry pilaf (see right)

A day in advance, put the fillet of beef in an enamel or earthenware bowl. Whisk together the cherry brandy, red wine, garlic, bay leaves, thyme, peppercorns, coriander seeds and pour over the beef. Cover and refrigerate for at least 12 hours, turning 2-3 times.

Remove the fillet from the marinade and pat it dry with kitchen paper. Coat the bottom of a heavy frying-pan with olive oil, sprinkle it evenly with salt and heat until just before the smoking point. Sear the fillet well on all sides, which shouldn't take more than a total of 3-4 minutes. Set it on a rack in a roasting tin.

Preheat an oven to 230°C (450°F, gas 8). About 40 minutes or so before you want to serve the beef, put it in the oven and roast for 25 minutes – until the juices run pink when you puncture the meat with a skewer. I like my meat rare, but if you don't, continue – probably to 40 minutes. Remove the roast to a warmed serving platter and let it rest for a few minutes in a warm spot, such as in front of the open oven door, allowing the juices to retreat to the centre of the meat.

Meanwhile deglaze the roasting pan with the strained marinade and boil until reduced by half. Carve the roast, pour the pan juices over the meat, and serve with cherry pilaf.

PILÁFI-VÍSINO

CHERRY PILAF

In Greece this is made with 75 g (3 oz) dried sour cherries, soaked in 125 ml (4 fl oz) apple or orange juice. You can try it with raisins, prunes or dried apricots, or with fresh or canned cherries as given in the recipe.

SERVES 4-6

350 g (12 oz) Basmati or long-grain rice
150 g (5 oz) onion, chopped
5 tablespoons fruity olive oil
tops and leaves of 4-6 celery stalks, chopped or 65 g (2½ oz) flat leaf parsley, chopped
175 g (6 oz) fresh Morellos, or drained, canned cherries, with 50 ml (2 fl oz) juice
75 g (3 oz) walnuts, chopped
salt and freshly ground black pepper

Put the rice in a sieve and rinse under running water until it runs clear. Put the rice in a bowl, cover with water and leave to soak for at least 30 minutes. Drain well before you use it.

In a saucepan large enough to take the pilaf, heat 3 tablespoons oil and add the onions. Fry gently until transparent. Add 2 more spoonfuls of oil, the celery and rice and stir until the rice becomes translucent.

Stone the cherries, reserving the juice. Add the cherries and walnuts, season with salt and pepper and sauté for 1-2 minutes. Add the cherry juice (replacing part of the water, if you are using canned cherries) and 650 ml (1 pt 2 fl oz) water. Cover and simmer over low heat for about 20 minutes – until craters form on the surface and the rice is *al dente*.

Remove from the heat, stretch a piece of muslin or a clean tea towel over the top, cover with the lid and set aside for 15-20 minutes to steam. Serve with the beef.

MERCHANT'S HOUSE *Imposing mansions, or* archontiká, *bear witness to prosperous times in previous centuries.*

HIRINÓ PSITÓ ME NERÁNTZIA

ROAST PORK LOIN WITH SEVILLE ORANGE GLAZE AND OLIVES

This recipe was inspired by those things provided by the island landscape which are a perfect foil for a rich pork roast – the olive and the bitter orange. In the absence of Seville oranges, try substituting sweet orange and lemon juice. I serve this with turnips sautéed with greens (*see page 66*).

SERVES 6

*1.8 kg (4 lb) pork loin on the bone, skinned,
trimmed, rolled and tied*

*150 g (5 oz) throúmbes or other Greek olives
in brine*

3 garlic cloves, one of them whole

about 75 ml (3 fl oz) oúzo

½ teaspoon salt

½ teaspoon dried mountain thyme (see page 16)

1 teaspoon honey

2 oranges (Seville or sweet) sliced, to garnish

MARINADE

*4-5 Seville (bitter) oranges, or 2-3 sweet oranges
and 2 lemons*

2 tablespoons honey

2-3 garlic cloves, finely chopped

1 teaspoon mountain thyme (see page 16)

½ teaspoon salt

At least a day in advance, rinse the olives in cold water and remove the stones. Put the flesh in a jar with a garlic clove and pour in *oúzo* to cover.

A day in advance, put the pork loin in a bowl or earthenware dish. Using a potato peeler, remove strips of zest from 2 oranges and reserve. Squeeze the oranges (and lemons, if using), until you have 250 ml (8 fl oz) juice. Mix this with all the other marinade ingredients and pour over the pork. Cover and refrigerate, turning the roast several times.

The day of the roast, allow the pork to come to room temperature. Cut the reserved orange zest into julienne shreds and blanch in boiling water for

5 minutes. Rinse then reserve.

Remove the pork from the marinade and pat it dry. Mix together 2 finely chopped garlic cloves with the salt, thyme and honey and massage this into the pork. Put it, fat side up, in a roasting tin.

In an oven preheated to 200°C (400°F, gas 6) roast for 1 hour 20 minutes to 1 hour 30 minutes, basting with the pan juices about every 10 minutes. After the first 45 minutes, add the strained marinade to the pan juices, and continue basting every 10 minutes. For the last 10 minutes baste with the *oúzo* in which the olives were macerated. The pork is done when the juices run clear, when it is pierced.

Remove the pork to a serving platter and keep warm. Skim all the fat from the roasting tin, add the orange julienne and boil to reduce the liquid by half.

Carve the pork and return the meat to the warmed platter. Decorate with oranges. Pour the sauce over the meat and sprinkle with the drained olives.

HIRINÓ ME KYTHÓNIA

PORK WITH QUINCE

Quince is a forgotten fruit which deserves to be remembered and relished. Although quinces were enjoyed raw in ancient times, they have a tartness which many people today find distasteful. They are wonderful poached, baked, or in tarts and pies, and their acidity provides a nice foil to heavy meat dishes. The longer they are cooked, the pinker the flesh becomes.

Piglets and quinces ripen at the same time. Stewed together they are like the autumn air – heavy as the falling leaves and fresh as the lifting heat. Conference pears can be used, but they produce an altogether sweeter dish. If you use them, reduce the pear quantity to 1.1 kg (2 lb) and the sugar to 25 g (1 oz).

SERVES 6-7

1 kg (2 lb) pork, shoulder or leg meat,
cut into 2.5-4 cm (1-1½ in) cubes
1 large mild Spanish onion, chopped
4 tablespoons fruity olive oil
½ teaspoon freshly ground cumin
½ teaspoon freshly ground cinnamon
¼ teaspoon cayenne
¼ teaspoon freshly ground black pepper
2 medium-sized leeks, trimmed, washed and whites
thinly sliced
1.4 kg (3 lb) quinces, peeled, cored and sliced
125 g (4 oz) sugar
15 g (½ oz) flat leaf parsley, finely chopped
2 tablespoons finely chopped fresh dill
½ fat bunch of spring onions, white and
light green chopped

In a flameproof casserole big enough to take all the ingredients, heat 2 tablespoons olive oil. Sauté the onion until brown, then sprinkle with the cumin, cinnamon, cayenne and black pepper and continue frying for a minute.

Add the pork cubes and sauté until well browned on all sides. Pour in 250 ml (8 fl oz) water, cover and simmer gently for about an hour, adding more water as necessary.

In the meantime, heat 2 tablespoons oil in a saucepan and fry the leeks gently until transparent. Add the cubed quince and stir, adding a little water if the fruit sticks. Sprinkle with the sugar and let it caramelize – about 20 minutes. When the pork has had an hour and a half, add the quince mixture and simmer until meat and fruit are tender – another 30 minutes or so.

Garnish with parsley, dill and spring onions and serve with rice or pasta.

SUN-BATHING ON PAROS *Pigs take a rest in the sun.*

YOUVARLÁKIA

MEATBALLS WITH RICE IN GARLIC AND TOMATO SAUCE

These earthy meatballs have a seasoning typical of *soutzoukákia*, or Smyrna sausages.

MAKES ABOUT 20

500 g (1 lb) minced beef
100 g (4 oz) grated onion
3 garlic cloves, finely chopped
½ teaspoon oregano
1 teaspoon ground cumin
2 tablespoons finely chopped flat leaf parsley
2 tablespoons finely chopped fresh mint
½ teaspoon freshly ground black pepper
salt
50 g (2 oz) long-grain rice
4 tablespoons fruity olive oil

TOMATO SAUCE

100 g (4 oz) onion, finely chopped
4 garlic cloves, finely chopped
½ teaspoon freshly ground cinnamon
1 tablespoon honey
1 kg (2 lb) tomatoes, skinned, seeded and flesh chopped
salt and freshly ground black pepper
125 ml (4 fl oz) herb broth (see page 37) or water
2 tablespoons finely chopped flat leaf parsley
2 tablespoons finely chopped fresh mint
1 tablespoon finely chopped fresh basil

Put the minced beef in a bowl with the grated onion, garlic, oregano, cumin, parsley, mint and pepper and add salt. Rinse then scald the rice by pouring boiling water over it in a bowl; leave to soak for 5 minutes. Drain and add to the beef and mix all the ingredients well. Form small sausage shapes.

Heat the oil in a large heavy frying-pan and fry the meatballs until brown. Drain on kitchen paper.

Add the onion to the oil remaining in the pan and fry over gentle heat until transparent. Add the garlic, cinnamon and honey and stir until caramelized. Add the tomato, season and simmer for about 15 minutes until the sauce has reduced. Add 125 ml (4 fl oz) of herb broth or water and the meatballs. Cover and simmer for 30 minutes. Sprinkle with herbs.

KOTÓPOULO ME SÝKA

CHICKEN WITH FIGS IN RED WINE

This dish has been served on hot nights in the garden with the moon filtering through the almond trees. It goes quite well with ghost stories.

SERVES 4

1.6 kg (3½ lb) chicken, skinned, excess fat removed and cut into pieces, giblets reserved
1 teaspoon freshly ground coriander seed
¼ teaspoon cayenne pepper
½ teaspoon ground cumin
½ teaspoon ground black pepper
salt
175 g (6 oz) onions, thinly sliced
6-10 garlic cloves, whole (to taste)
2 bay leaves
10 fresh figs
250 ml (8 fl oz) mavrotháphne or ruby port
finely grated zest and juice of 1 lemon (to taste)
15 g (½ oz) flat leaf parsley, finely chopped

Arrange the chicken pieces and giblets in a heavy roasting dish. Sprinkle with the spices and salt and massage into the flesh. Distribute the onions, garlic, bay leaves and figs over and between the chicken pieces, pour in the wine and cover.

Cook in an oven preheated to 180°C (350°F, gas 4) for about 50 minutes, until the chicken is barely tender. Stir in the lemon zest and juice and return to the oven until almost falling from the bones – another 10-15 minutes. If there is an excess of liquid, leave off the cover for this part of the cooking. Sprinkle with parsley and serve with saffron rice (*see page 91*).

CAFÉ ON CRETE *Customers take refuge from the summer sun.*

KOTÓPOULO ME SÝKA (*overleaf*)

KOTÓPOULO TIS SKÁRAS

GRILLED CHICKEN WITH HERBS UNDER THE SKIN

In ancient Greece, chickens were valued mainly for their eggs. On islands where commercial chickens are not yet distributed, this remains the case. I stopped at the house of a family from whom I used to buy beautiful brown, fresh eggs. Kirio Lefteri answered the door and told me, 'No eggs today'. I said, 'Tomorrow then?' He said, 'No'. I asked 'When?' He said, 'Never'. I asked 'Why?' and he replied, 'because we ate the chickens …' This recipe is not the ideal way to cook an older fowl, but a tender little broiler, on an early summer evening after a swim, would be perfect. It is delicious with the *prassórizo*, saffron rice with leeks (*see page* 59), or turnips sautéed with greens (*see page* 66).

SERVES 4

*1.4 kg (3 lb) chicken, excess fat removed,
quartered and without backbone*
25 g (1 oz) flat leaf parsley, finely chopped
25 g (1 oz) fresh fennel leaves, finely chopped
*½ fat bunch spring onions, 40 g (1½ oz) white
and pale green finely chopped*
*2 tablespoons thick yogurt, or sour cream
or crème fraîche*
salt and freshly ground black pepper
1 teaspoon olive oil

Combine the parsley, fennel, onions, yogurt, salt, pepper and olive oil in a bowl, with seasoning, so they are evenly mixed. Push your fingers between the skin and the flesh to make a cavity right across each portion. Scoop up about a quarter of the herb mixture in your fingers and shove under the chicken skin, pushing it in gently until all parts of the flesh are covered. Massage the chicken to get the herbs evenly distributed under the skin. Put the chicken aside to marinate for a good 30 minutes – the longer the better. (The recipe can be done ahead to this point.)

Grill for about 30 minutes, turning once, until the chicken is brown and the juices run clear when the flesh is pierced.

GALÓPOULO FASÓLIA

TURKEY IN RED WINE WITH BEANS AND WILD MUSHROOMS

Island turkeys live up the mountain with the goats and sheep, feeding on herbs and strolling under pine trees whose fallen needles protect wild mushrooms – their partners in the pot. They are rather scrawny animals – they don't have huge white breasts and there is a definite wildness in their darkened meat. The nearest equivalent is a free-range turkey with mountain herbs, wild mushrooms and imagination.

Serve this with crusty bread and a big bowl of boiled greens, dressed with lemon and olive oil.

SERVES 8 OR 10

*4 kg (9 lb) free-range turkey with giblets,
a hen if possible, cleaned and cut
into 8 or 10 portions*
*175 g (6 oz) haricot beans, soaked overnight
in cold water to cover*
*500 g (1 lb) wild mushrooms such as chanterelles,
cleaned (see page 35), or the same weight
of button mushrooms plus 25-40 g (1-1½ oz)
dried ceps or morels, soaked*
6-7 tablespoons fruity olive oil
5 cloves garlic, finely chopped
350 g (12 oz) onions, finely chopped
1 bay leaf, crushed
*1 tablespoon fresh thyme or ½ teaspoon dried
mountain thyme (see page 16)*
1½ teaspoons fresh rosemary or ½ teaspoon dried
½ teaspoon finely grated orange zest
salt and freshly ground black pepper
450 ml (16 fl oz) red wine
1 tablespoon semolina (optional)
25 g (1 oz) flat leaf parsley

Drain the beans and put them in a saucepan with cold water to cover. Bring to the boil and simmer for 10 minutes. Drain the beans in a colander and rinse under running water. Return to the pan and cover with fresh water. Bring to the boil and simmer for 1-1½ hours, adding a small amount of water when necessary, until they are tender. Drain, salt to taste and reserve (this can be done ahead).

Slice fresh mushrooms (and soak dried ones, if using). In a heavy frying-pan heat 2 tablespoons of olive oil and sauté the fresh mushrooms with 2 chopped garlic cloves for 3-5 minutes – until they give up some of their juices. Reserve the pan off the heat.

Choose a large flameproof casserole big enough to hold the turkey and the beans. Heat 3 tablespoons olive oil and sauté the turkey pieces and giblets (reserving the liver to cook later) until well-browned on all sides. You may have to do this in two or three batches, so the pieces are not too crowded. Remove the turkey to a platter as you go.

Add 1-2 tablespoons olive oil to the casserole and sauté the onion until amber-coloured, stirring in splashes of water as needed, to prevent sticking and burning. Stir in the rest of the garlic, the bay leaf, thyme, rosemary, grated orange zest, a seasoning of salt and pepper and finally the wine. Add 350ml (12 fl oz) water and bring gently to the boil.

Add the fried turkey and giblets. Cover and simmer for about 1½ hours. Check the liquid from time to time, adding water if necessary.

Add the beans and fried mushrooms. If using dried mushrooms, rinse these well and strain the juice, then add both. Cook for another 30 minutes until the turkey is nice and tender. About 5-10 minutes before the end of cooking time add the chopped turkey livers. If there is too much liquid for your taste, sprinkle in the semolina and simmer another 5-10 minutes until the sauce thickens. Taste and adjust the seasoning, sprinkle with parsley and serve.

GRAZING GOATS AND SHEEP *A shepherd watches over his animals in the late afternoon sun.*

KOTÓPOULO ME ANTZOÚYES

CHICKEN WITH SUN-DRIED TOMATOES AND ANCHOVIES

Take yourself back a hundred years to a stone farmhouse in winter. An impudent chicken cackles outside the kitchen door; the larder is hung with strings of dried tomatoes and lined with earthenware jars of capers, pickled anchovies, pine nuts and much more. All the ingredients for this dish are at hand.

SERVES 4-5

1-1¼ kg (2½-3 lb) chicken, excess fat removed, and cut into pieces
200 g (7 oz) onions, thinly sliced
2 tablespoons fruity olive oil
¼ teaspoon freshly ground clove
¼ teaspoon freshly ground coriander seeds
½ teaspoon freshly ground black pepper
2 teaspoons honey
50 g (2 oz) can anchovies, rinsed and dried
10 cloves scorthostoúmbi, pickled garlic (see page 25), finely chopped
about 30 sun-dried tomatoes (in oil, or soaked in 250 ml [8 fl oz] boiling water)
2 tablespoons capers
75 g (3 oz) pine nuts, lightly toasted
salt
15 g (½ oz) flat leaf parsley, chopped

In a flameproof casserole, heat the olive oil and fry the onions gently until transparent. Add the chicken pieces and brown well on all sides. Sprinkle with the clove, coriander, pepper and honey, then stir, adding some of the tomato liquid if it starts to stick.

Use a mortar and pestle or a food processor to make a smooth paste of the anchovies and garlic, and stir into the chicken sauce. Add the tomatoes and 250 ml (8 fl oz) soaking liquid or water. Simmer for about 45 minutes, adding more liquid, if necessary.

Stir in the capers and pine nuts, and continue simmering for another 10 minutes, until the chicken is very tender. Taste and add salt. Transfer to a heated platter, sprinkle with parsley and serve.

ORTÍKIA STA KLIMATÓFYLLA

QUAIL IN VINE LEAVES

In autumn during the hunting season, there are more hunters and hunting dogs on the islands than birds. Those first crisp days, hunters swagger up the mountain with their chests puffed up beneath new military surplus fatigues and rifles slung over their shoulders. They are the legions of local men in hot pursuit of the last two quail and single partridge left on the island.

'Naughty Noti', my neighbour, used to return with a bag of hórta, wild greens, rather than come home empty-handed, even though it is a strictly female practice to pick these. I prefer to buy my game birds in Athens, at the bird market, where they come from special farms. I roast them over the embers outside and serve them with the grilled aubergine on page 65.

SERVES 4

4 plump quails, freshly killed and dressed
1 teaspoon honey
grated zest of 1 lemon, with 1 teaspoon juice
1 tablespoon dried mountain thyme (see page 16)
2-3 tablespoons fruity olive oil
salt and freshly ground black pepper
4 tablespoons cognac
8-12 vine leaves (see page 86)

In a small bowl, mix together the honey, lemon, thyme, olive oil, salt and pepper. Massage this mixture into the skin of each bird. Put them aside in a cool place to marinate for 2-3 hours, or overnight in the refrigerator.

Heat 1 tablespoon cognac in a ladle over a small flame. Light it and pour it over one bird, repeating for the others. Wrap each quail in grape leaves, securing them with a toothpick.

Bake them in a roasting tin in an oven preheated to 180°C (350°F, gas 4). They should take 30 minutes.

ORTÍKIA STA KLIMATÓFYLLA

KOUNÉLI KE VERÍKOKO ME PLIGOÚRI

RABBIT AND APRICOTS WITH CRACKED WHEAT

This recipe of my own invention was inspired by ingredients which have always been provided by the Greek landscape. It is combined with timeless cooking traditions to approximate what might have been.

SERVES 6

*1.4-1.5 kg (3-3¼ lb) rabbit,
dressed and cut into pieces
4 tablespoons fruity olive oil
500 g (1 lb) onions, thinly sliced
1 teaspoon of honey
tops and leaves of 6 celery stalks, chopped
½ teaspoon mountain thyme (see page 16)
1 bay leaf, crumbled
1 teaspoon freshly ground coriander seed
½ teaspoon freshly ground black pepper
salt
1-2 crystals of mastíhi, pulverized with mortar and
pestle, or 1 tablespoon mastíha liquor,
or 1 tablespoon oúzo
175 g (6 oz) dried apricots, soaked overnight in
425 ml (¾ pt) water, then puréed in a blender with
a little of the soaking water
1 tablespoon scorthostoúmbi, garlic vinegar
(see page 25)
pligoúri, cracked wheat (see right) to serve*

In a heavy frying-pan (which must not be aluminium) heat 3 tablespoons olive oil and brown the rabbit pieces on all sides. Remove the rabbit.

Add the remaining tablespoon of oil. Fry the onions gently until translucent. Stir in the honey, celery, thyme, bay leaf, coriander, pepper, salt and *mastíha* powder or liquor. Add the apricot pulp, season and simmer for 2-3 minutes.

Return the rabbit pieces to the pan with any escaped juices, cover and simmer for 30 minutes. Add the *scorthostoúmbi*, with a little water if necessary. Cover and continue simmering for 30-35 minutes – until tender. Serve with *pligoúri*, cracked wheat.

WATCHING THE DAY GO BY *A woman sits peacefully on her terrace, shaded by the vine growing above.*

PLIGOÚRI

CRACKED WHEAT

*275 g (10 oz) cracked wheat
2 tablespoons olive oil
salt and freshly ground black pepper*

Bring 700 ml (1 pt 4 fl oz) salted water to the boil. Sprinkle in the cracked wheat and add the oil. Cover tightly and simmer over a very low heat for about 15 minutes – until tender. You may have to add a tiny bit of water, but be careful, as it easily turns to mush.

Season with pepper, taste (and add salt if needed) and fluff with a fork. Stretch a piece of cheesecloth or muslin or a tea towel over the top, replace the lid and set aside in a warm place for 15-20 minutes, so the steam can be absorbed and the grains separate.

120

PÉRDIKES ME SÝKA

PARTRIDGES WITH DRIED FIGS

If you have access to an area outdoors, do the preliminary cooking of the birds over glowing juniper embers – grilling about 10-12 minutes each side – before stewing them.

Serve with lots of country bread and a tomato and *róka*, rocket salad.

SERVES 4

*2 partridges, about 500 g (1 lb) each, with livers reserved (see below) and gizzards,
or those from 1 chicken*
2 tablespoons olive oil
*½ teaspoon scorthostoúmbi, garlic vinegar
(see page 25)*
½ teaspoon oúzo
¼ teaspoon salt
¼ teaspoon dried mountain thyme (see page 16)

STOCK
*10-12 dried figs, 175 g (6 oz) if they are not
ready-plumped*
450 ml (16 fl oz) red wine
2 tablespoons oúzo
½ teaspoon dried mountain thyme
2 bay leaves
2 juniper berries
2½ shallots
*8 cloves scorthostoúmbi, (see page 25),
plus ½ teaspoon of juice from the jar*
salt and freshly ground black pepper

TO FINISH
½ shallot, very finely chopped
2 partridge livers, or 1 chicken liver
½ teaspoon olive oil
4 slices wholemeal bread, toasted

Split the partridges in half and remove all the bones except the drumsticks and wing bones. Snip off the wing tips and flatten each partridge half, pressing them with the side of a heavy kitchen knife, and place them on a platter.

Beat the olive oil with garlic vinegar, *oúzo*, salt and dried thyme. Pour this over the flattened birds, being sure to coat both sides, and set them aside to macerate.

In a stock pan put the birds' bones and trimmings (but not livers) and gizzard(s) with the figs, wine, *oúzo*, thyme, bay leaves, juniper berries, shallots and pickled garlic and add 250 ml (8 fl oz) water. Bring them to the boil, then cover and simmer very slowly for 1-1½ hours, until the figs are plump and soft and the stock is reduced and of good flavour.

Remove and discard the bones. Remove and reserve all but 2 figs. Strain the stock, then mash all the remaining ingredients to a rough purée. Reserve 2 teaspoons of this purée. Stir the rest back into the strained liquid, with the vinegar, and reserve.

If possible, grill the partridges over juniper embers (see above). Otherwise sauté them, with some of the marinade in a pan until they are browned on both sides.

Place the bird halves in a saucepan big enough to hold them in one layer, fit in the figs and pour in the reserved juices. Cover and simmer for 35-40 minutes (or for 15-20 minutes if they were grilled over charcoal), until the birds are tender and the sauce has reduced. Taste and season with salt and pepper.

To serve, chop the shallots and liver together. Mix with ½ teaspoon olive oil and the reserved fig purée. Spread this mixture on 4 pieces of toast and grill until the liver mixture bubbles.

Place a half partridge on each piece of toast, flank with 2 reserved figs and pour the sauce round them on each plate.

SWEET THINGS

*Fruit is the traditional conclusion to a
meal in Greece, and there are abundant
opportunities throughout the day to enjoy a
delicate pastry or hearty slice of cake.*

PORTOKÁLIA SE MAVROTHÁPNE *above* (p. 125),
ACHLÁTHIA STO FOÚRNO *left* (p. 125),
RIZÓGALO ME SÁLTSA VERÍKOKO *right* (p. 130)

I WAS WALKING ONE DAY on the outskirts of Hydra.
Next to the dark green foliage of a wild carob tree,
a baby donkey tottered on his spindly legs, inviting me
to pet him with his huge, dark eyes, and was as frisky
as my puppy with whom he played. We continued on,
followed by the young mongrel, the baby donkey,
closely pursued by his mother and joined by a stray dog
and a curious cat. It occured to me that I only needed
a goat to make a truly ecumenical group.

The bells of the little chapel on the other side of an
old stone ruin rang out eagerly as a woman I had never
seen before, arms full of flowers, signalled to me. The
freshly whitewashed church was festooned with flags,
flowers and well wishers. It was the name day of Agios
Nikolaos, patron of sailors, small children and this
chapel. The woman was excited because she didn't
know me and it is good luck to have a stranger at the
name day ceremony of a church. I was wondering how
she felt about my entourage when the village priest
emerged. He blessed the animals and suggested it was
rather too crowded inside for them.

After the service, everyone gathered in the *salóni*,
or living room, of the woman with the flowers. She
lived next door and was responsible for the church, her
great-grandfather having built it in gratitude for being
saved at sea. There are many island chapels dedicated
to St Nicholas for this same reason.

The walls in the *salóni* were lined with chairs, with
all the women seated along one side of the room and
the men along the other side. Small children and the
priest moved back and forth while the hostess and her
sisters served coffee, sweet liqueurs, brandy and
sweets. There was true conviviality despite the
regimented arrangements. The liqueurs were made
mostly of fruits and some flowers. Rose liqueur was a
favourite, and there was cherry and apricot brandy
which the priest seemed to like quite well. It was
nearing Christmas so there were *melomakárona*, honey

cakes, and *kourambiéthes*, buttery almond crescents,
both of which are traditional at this time. Homemade
baklavá and a vast selection of *glyka tou koutalioú*,
spoon sweets, completed the feast.

Spoon sweets should comprise a category of sweets
unto themselves. They are preserves served in a
glykothíki, which is a silver or brass egg-shaped holder
with a row of spoons hanging round the outside. As the
glykothíki is passed, each guest is given a glass of cold
water. He or she takes a spoon and removes a portion
of the sweet, savours it and puts the spoon into the
glass, flavouring the water with the syrupy vestiges.
These spoon sweets are made from whole green bitter
oranges, ripe bitter oranges, quince, pumpkin, unripe
walnuts, aubergines and all the normal fruits. They are
usually the whole fruit or bite-sized pieces preserved in
sugar or honey syrup. Sweet syrups are also made of
most fruits and mixed with ice cold water to make a
refreshing drink. *Soumátha*, made of almond milk,
used to be served at engagement ceremonies. I have
served it to Greeks who have never tasted it, which is
a shame. It is pure poetry. *Visinátha* is a bright red, sour
cherry syrup – a favourite with children. Peach syrup
could make you swoon and *aravosykosyrópi*, or prickly
pear syrup, is mysteriously refreshing.

Visits from house to house for religious, social or
personal reasons are an integral part of Greek life.
Preserves, cakes, biscuits, syrups, liqueurs and coffee
are essential to these daily rituals, woven as they are
into the fabric of daily island life, as something is
always offered to a visitor. The preparation of sweets
also involves a measure of ritual, as families of women
will spend days together picking and preserving fruit or
making special pastries for weddings, christenings and
name days. Made sweets are rarely served after meals.
Since ancient times the preferred dessert has always
been fresh fruit, of which there is a delicious
abundance on the islands.

ACHLÁTHIA STO FOÚRNO

PEARS BAKED IN SAMOS WINE WITH ORANGE ZEST AND PISTACHIOS

The pears usually cooked in this way are juicy green musk-flavoured pears called *crystálli*. As there are thousands of varieties of this versatile fruit in the world, I can do no more than recommend a firm, green, well-perfumed pear.

You should be able to find skinned unsalted pistachios in Middle Eastern shops and some supermarkets. If not, plunge in boiling water for 2 minutes, and pop from their skins.

SERVES 6

6 green pears, about 150-200 g (5-7 oz) each
1 lemon
finely grated zest of 1 orange
50 g (2 oz) sugar
75 g (3 oz) unsalted pistachio nuts, skinned and roughly chopped
250 ml (8 fl oz) Samos or other muscat wine

Peel the pears, leaving the stems intact, and sprinkle a little lemon juice over each one.

Mix the orange zest, sugar and chopped pistachios together in a bowl. Place the pears close together in an earthenware or ovenproof glass dish and sprinkle the nut mixture over them. Pour in the wine.

Cover the dish with foil and bake in an oven preheated to 180°C (350°F, gas 4) for about 30 minutes or until tender. Remove from the oven and cool. If you like the syrup thick, drain it into a small saucepan and boil to reduce it to the required consistency, then pour back over the pears.

PORTOKÁLIA SE MAVROTHÁPHNE

ORANGES IN RED WINE

In winter, in Greece, it is often warmer outside than inside. When the thick stone walls and floors insinuate their chilly dampness through to the bone, it is good to go out for a walk. When you return, it is time for a cup of tea by the fire with a juicy plate of these dazzling oranges and a chunk of earthy goat's cheese melted over a slice of country bread.

SERVES 6

8 navel oranges
125 g (4½ oz) sugar
450 ml (16 fl oz) mavrotháphne (see page 17)
or ruby port
1 bay leaf
1 clove

Remove the zest of 2 of the oranges with a zester; or pare finely with a potato peeler, then cut into thin julienne strips. With a very sharp knife, cut off the skin and outside membrane of all the oranges, so you have glistening orbs of golden pulp. Do this over a bowl to catch escaping juice.

Choose a saucepan just large enough to hold 2 oranges at a time and put in the escaped juice and remaining ingredients. Dissolve the sugar and simmer for 5 minutes. Submerge 2 oranges at a time and cook just long enough to warm them through – about 3 minutes. If they bob up, place a small weighted saucer over them. Remove to a serving dish and continue with the next pair until finished.

Boil to reduce the syrup by half, drizzle over the oranges and chill.

GRANÍTA ROTHÁKINO

PEACH SORBET

I serve sorbet all day, all summer long. Children and sweet-loving adults don't realize they are simply eating fresh fruit in a slightly altered form.

SERVES 8

1-1.3 kg (2-3 lb) fresh, almost over-ripe peaches, or nectarines
1 orange
1 teaspoon cognac
2-4 tablespoons caster sugar
⅛ teaspoon rosewater (optional)

GRANÍTA ROTHÁKINO

Peel the peaches and stone them. Cut the flesh into pieces and purée in a food processor or through a vegetable mill. Measure the results: you need about 1.2 litres (2 pt) purée. Mix in 50 ml (2 fl oz) orange juice and the cognac and stir in sugar to taste. The rosewater will give a more oriental taste.

Pour the purée into a flat-bottomed metal container and put in the coldest part of your freezer. Every 20-30 minutes stir with a fork to break up the ice crystals that form round the edge. When the sorbet is hard, return to the processor long enough to soften and break up the crystals. Serve, or return to the freezer, where it should stay soft enough to serve straight away.

GRANÍTA PEPÓNI

MELON SORBET

All of Athens used to spend summer evenings in cafés savouring conversations and ices chosen from endless lists. Fifteen years ago we had a choice of two flavours in our island cafés. Today my neighbours are incredulous when I offer them the forgotten delights of *granita*. I like to use over-ripe fruit for my sorbet, as it has a stronger perfume.

SERVES 8-10

2-3 ripe honeydews, or any other melon, seeded
1 grapefruit (for green-fleshed melons) or
1 orange (for pink-fleshed melons)
1 teaspoon oúzo, or any other anise-flavoured liquor
1 teaspoon (or more) lemon juice
2-4 tablespoons caster sugar

Cut the flesh of the melons into chunks and purée in a food processor, or through a vegetable mill. Measure the results: you need about 1.2 litres (2 pt) purée.

Squeeze the grapefruit or orange, adding 50 ml (2 fl oz) juice to the melon purée, with the *oúzo* and lemon juice. Taste and add sugar (and more lemon juice) if needed: freezing diminishes flavour.

Pour all this into a metal container (metal conducts the cold better) and place in the coldest part of your freezer. Stir with a fork every 20-30 minutes, breaking up the crystals round the edge, until it hardens. When the sorbet is hard, process it again in the food processor, just long enough to break up the ice crystals, and serve (or return to the freezer). It shouldn't become too hard again.

SÝKA STO FOÚRNO

BAKED FIGS

I call the 'dog days' of summer 'fig days' on the Greek islands. Mine are taken up making fig brandy, fig jam, fig chutney, dried figs, preserved figs, fig cakes, fig tarts and begging passers-by to pick some figs. When I took some to Kiria Eleftheria, she told me that her grandmother used to bake them with sesame seeds and slivered *nerantzákia*, preserved, green bitter oranges.

I serve these for breakfast, tea or dessert, hot or cold, sprinkled with the almonds and accompanied by a bowl of thick yogurt. They keep in the refrigerator for 10 days if you have a tree and want to make mountains of them.

SERVES 8

24 ripe figs, Smyrna or your choice
65 g (2½ oz) blanched almonds, slivered or chopped
2 tablespoons honey
finely grated zest of 1 lemon plus 1 tablespoon juice
50 ml (2 fl oz) cognac
2 bay leaves

Spread the blanched almonds on a baking sheet and toast them in an oven preheated to 150°C (300°F, gas 2) for 7-10 minutes, until lightly golden.

Put the figs in an ovenproof glass or earthenware casserole. Whisk the honey, lemon juice and cognac together and pour over the figs. Sprinkle them with the lemon zest and nestle the bay leaves among the fruits. Cover and bake in an oven preheated to 180°C (350°F, gas 4) for 20-25 minutes. Serve sprinkled with almonds.

SIPHNÓPITTA

FRESH SPRING CHEESECAKE

This is a speciality of the island Siphnos, where it is made for *Tirini*, cheese week, the last week before Lent. If you prefer a richer version, use *manoúri* or cream cheese instead of *mizíthra*, which is a whey cheese (*see page 11*).

SERVES 6-8

700 g (1½ lb) fresh mizíthra *cheese (see page 11)*
or cottage cheese, sieved, or ricotta
4 medium-sized eggs
1 teaspoon vinegar (for the bowl)
175 ml (6 fl oz) honey
finely grated zest of 1 orange,
plus 2 tablespoons juice
1 pinch cream of tartar
1 tablespoon icing sugar
1 tablespoon icing sugar mixed with 1 teaspoon
freshly ground cinnamon

PASTRY

350 g (12 oz) plain flour, plus extra for kneading
1 tablespoon icing sugar
½ teaspoon baking powder
1 pinch of salt
grated zest of 1 lemon
125 ml (4 fl oz) olive oil
125 ml (4 fl oz) mavróthaphne *(see page 17),*
ruby port or other sweet wine

FLOATING MARKET *Sun-ripened fruit from across the water is sold directly from a* caïque *in the port of Aegina.*

Start by making the pastry. Sift the flour, icing sugar, baking powder and salt into a bowl. Mix in the lemon zest and make a well in the centre. Pour the oil and wine into the well and mix with a wooden spoon until well incorporated. Turn onto a floured work surface and knead 5-7 minutes, adding flour if necessary to make soft, smooth dough. Cover and put aside for an hour or two to relax.

Break the pastry into two-thirds, and one-third portions. Roll out the larger portion to a circle 38-40 cm (15-16 in) in diameter. Oil a 23 cm (9 in) push-bottom spring-release cake tin and fit in the pastry in the bottom and up the sides, letting the excess hang out. Roll out the remaining pastry to a rectangle as wide as the cake tin and about 8 mm (⅓ in) thick. Cut into strips.

For the filling separate the eggs, putting 4 yolks and 2 whites in a large bowl. Put the remaining 2 whites in a smaller bowl which has been wiped with a cloth dampened with vinegar. Beat the egg yolks and whites with the honey and grated orange zest and juice until golden and slightly frothy.

To lighten the cheese, beat it with a wooden spoon, or put it in a food processor for a few seconds. Beat in the egg mixture. (If you are using a food processor, please don't overprocess the mixture, or you risk separation during baking.)

Whisk the egg whites with the cream of tartar. As they form soft peaks add the icing sugar and continue whisking until stiff, shiny peaks form. Gingerly fold the egg whites into the cheese mixture.

Fill the pastry case with the cheese mixture. Place the pastry strips over the top, criss-crossing them in a basket-weave pattern. Crimp the edges attractively. Bake in an oven preheated to 180°C (350°F, gas 4) for 1-1½ hours, until the pastry is golden and a skewer comes out clean when the filling is pierced. (Cover the top with foil if it is browning too much.) Cool, then sprinkle with the sugar and cinnamon mixture.

KOLOKYTHÓPITTA

PUMPKIN PIE

Serve this pie as it is, or pass around a bowl of thick yogurt beaten with a teaspoon of sugar and a tablespoon of Cointreau.

SERVES 6-8

8-9 sheets filo pastry, 50 x 30 cm (20 x 12 in)
125-175 ml (4-6 fl oz) mild olive oil
1 teaspoon cracked wheat or raw rice

FILLING

1.8 kg (4 lb) pumpkin flesh (buy a pumpkin of over
2 kg [5 lb] for this)
grated zest and juice of 2 oranges
125 ml (4 fl oz) mild olive oil
125 g (4 oz) caster sugar
2 teaspoons freshly ground cinnamon
2 tablespoons semolina or cream of wheat
1 medium-sized egg, beaten
250 g (8 oz) walnuts, roughly chopped

SYRUP

350 g (12 oz) caster sugar
zest and juice of 1 orange
zest and juice of 1 lemon
2 tablespoons cognac

Start by making the syrup. Put the strips of grated zest into a small pan with 75 ml (3 fl oz) water and boil for 5 minutes. Add the orange and lemon juices and stir in the sugar. Cover and simmer for a further 5 minutes, until you have a clear syrup. Add the cognac, stir over heat a few times, and remove. Leave to chill overnight.

The next day make the filling. Cut the pumpkin into 2.5 cm (1 in) cubes and put them in a heavy-bottomed pot with the orange juice (having reserved the grated zest). Cook, covered, over very low heat, stirring occasionally, until tender – 30-40 minutes, depending on toughness. Cool and drain, reserving the liquid.

Whisk together the reserved liquid in a small saucepan with the olive oil, sugar, cinnamon and orange zest until the sugar has dissolved. Stir in the semolina and cook over low heat, stirring, until thickened. Pour this slowly onto the beaten egg in a bowl, stirring constantly. You should have a thick, smooth emulsion. Toss the pumpkin and chopped walnuts together, and stir them into the cinnamon/orange custard.

Keep the sheets of filo you are not using under a damp cloth to prevent them from drying out. Oil a 25 cm (10 in) push-bottom, spring-release cake tin. Brush one sheet of filo with oil, then lay it across the bottom of the cake tin and up the sides. Turn the tin by 60 degrees, and repeat until you have have laid down 6 sheets, and gone a full 360 degrees.

Sprinkle the bottom of the pan with a teaspoon of cracked wheat or raw rice and pour in the filling.

Cut the remaining sheets of filo in half, which should make them 30 x 25 cm (12 x 10 in). Lay a sheet on top of the pumpkin mixture, brush with oil, and trim to fit the shape of the pan with kitchen scissors. Repeat this 3 more times. Fold the hanging edges from the bottom layers over them and brush with olive oil.

Put 2 more layers, cut to fit the top, over this, brushing between and over them. Bake in an oven preheated to 180°C (350°F, gas 4) for about 45 minutes, until the crust is burnished gold and crunchy.

Cool for 10 minutes. Release the sides of the cake tin and slide the *pítta* onto a serving dish with a lip (so the syrup doesn't run everywhere). Pour the chilled syrup over the hot *pítta* and leave until cold.

RIZÓGALO ME SÁLTSA VERÍKOKO

RICE PUDDING WITH APRICOT SAUCE AND CANDIED VIOLETS

Pandias' grandmother was a child of the *belle époque*, named after a renowned ancient courtesan. On her farm in Kifisia she grew acres of violets to match her eyes. She always carried a fresh nosegay of the flowers, pinned them to her hats, strewed her salads with them, garnished platters of her famous woodcock with bunches that had been deep fried and candied them to toss over desserts. Here is Grandmother Aspasia's *rizógalo*.

SERVES 4-6

700 ml (1 pt 2 fl oz) milk
6 leaves lemon verbena or 2 strips lemon zest
2 tablespoons short-grain rice
½ teaspoon cornflour, mixed to a paste with 2 tablespoons milk
about 2 tablespoons sugar, to taste
candied violets for decoration

SAUCE

6 fresh apricots, stoned
2 tablespoons sugar
6 leaves lemon verbena or 2 strips lemon zest
¹/₁₆ teaspoon almond extract

Rinse a saucepan with cold water and pour in the milk. Add the verbena or lemon zest and rice and cook over a very low heat, stirring occasionally. When the mixture simmers, stir the dissolved cornflour into the rice.

As the pudding thickens, stir more frequently. When it is thick to your liking, add sugar to taste, remove the verbena leaves or lemon zest and transfer to individual serving bowls to chill.

For the sauce, purée the apricots in a processor or food mill. Dissolve the sugar with 3 tablespoons water in a saucepan. Simmer with the verbena leaves or lemon zest for 5 minutes. Remove the leaves or zest, stir into the apricot purée, with the almond extract, and chill. To serve, lap each bowl of rice pudding with the sauce and strew with candied violets.

AMYGTHALOTÁ

ALMOND PEARS OR CAKES

My brother and sister-in-law were married on a summer night, under the almond trees strung with little lights. Maria, the *koumbára*, matron of honour, passed out hundreds of beautiful, pear-shaped almond cakes which she and all the women in her family had lovingly made together.

MAKES ABOUT 30

500 g (1 lb) unblanched almonds
250 g (8 oz) caster sugar
15 g (½ oz) soft white breadcrumbs
2 medium-sized eggs
1 teaspoon orange flower water, or rosewater, plus extra for spraying or dipping
32 or more cloves
icing sugar to powder

Blanch the almonds by plunging them into boiling water for 1-2 minutes. Remove and slip off the skins. Using a food processor or blender, grind the almonds finely with 2 tablespoons of the sugar and the breadcrumbs.

Beat the eggs with the orange flower or rosewater. Add the mixture to the almonds and beat in, with the rest of the sugar. Knead to a smooth paste.

Break off pieces of paste (about 1-2 tablespoons) and shape into small 'pears'. Insert a clove in the top of each one, for the stem. Place them on an oiled or non-stick baking sheet. Bake in an oven preheated to 150°C (300°F, gas 2) for about 20 minutes – until lightly coloured.

The old method of finishing these is to dip them in orange flower or rosewater, when they are cold. I prefer to spray them lightly with an atomizer or spray bottle, and then coat them lightly with powdered sugar.

STENCILLED FAÇADE *Tomatoes dry in the sun against a wall decorated with traditional stencil patterns.*

130

REVANÍ

SEMOLINA CAKE

This dessert was named after a 16th-century Turkish poet. Soaked in lemon syrup, it is a truly sinful cake when served with whipped cream.

MAKES 16 SLICES

75 g (3 oz) plain flour
½ teaspoon baking powder
250 g (8 oz) fine semolina or cream of wheat
4 medium-sized eggs, separated
75 g (3 oz) caster sugar
125 ml (4 fl oz) olive oil
finely grated zest of 2 lemons
½ teaspoon almond extract
2 oranges, to make 125 ml (4 fl oz) juice
1 teaspoon vinegar (for the bowl)
$^1/_{16}$ teaspoon cream of tartar
50 g (2 oz) blanched, slivered almonds

SYRUP

175 g (6 oz) caster sugar
zest and juice of 2 lemons
¼ teaspoon almond extract

Make the syrup ahead. Combine the sugar, lemon zest and juice and 350 ml (12 fl oz) water in a saucepan. Bring to the boil, simmer for 5 minutes then add the almond extract. Remove and chill overnight.

Oil and then line with paper a 30cm (12 in) square cake tin, at least 7.5 cm (3 in) deep. Sift together the plain flour and baking powder then stir in the semolina. Beat the egg yolks, sugar, olive oil, lemon zest and almond extract together until pale and creamy. Beat in the flour mixture, splashing with orange juice to moisten it.

Wipe a bowl with a cloth moistened with vinegar then put in the egg whites. Whisk with cream of tartar until stiff peaks form, then fold into the batter. Pour into the prepared tin and sprinkle with the almonds.

Bake in an oven preheated to 180°C (350°F, gas 4) for about 45 minutes until golden brown. Remove from the oven and, while still hot, cut into squares. Slowly pour the chilled syrup over it.

CHRISTÓPSOMO TIS KIRÍAS ZÍNIS

KIRIA ZINIS' CHRISTMAS BREAD

Once a year, the kitchen of this lovely lady glows with teacups, wine glasses and dessert plates (these are her measures) full of fruit, raisins and aromatics, as she prepares the best Christmas bread in Greece. The recipe does require semolina flour or cream of wheat.

MAKES 3 LARGE LOAVES

650 g (1 lb 10 oz) semolina flour or cream of wheat
500 g (1 lb) caster sugar
3 tablespoons freshly ground cinnamon
1 tablespoon freshly ground anise seed
1 tablespoon freshly ground coriander seed
2 teaspoons freshly ground cloves
about 3 oranges
about 6 tangerines
350 g (12 oz) currants
175 g (6 oz) sultanas
250 ml (8 fl oz) mild olive oil

STARTER DOUGH

25 g (1 oz) dried yeast
125 ml (4 fl oz) hot water, just above body temperature to a testing finger
650 g (1 lb 10 oz) plain flour, plus extra for kneading

Make the flavouring addition first. Combine the semolina flour, sugar, cinnamon, anise, coriander seeds and cloves in a bowl and add the finely grated zests of the oranges and tangerines. Squeeze 300 ml (½ pt) mixed orange and tangerine juice. Use half this juice to soak the currants and sultanas for a minimum of 1 hour, preferably overnight. Put the remaining juice in a pan with the olive oil. Heat until almost boiling. Pour this into the bowl with the flour and spice mixture and stir. Cover and leave overnight until needed.

Next day, combine the dried yeast with ½ teaspoon sugar and the hot water in a cup. Put the flour in a bowl, making a well in the centre. Pour in the yeast. Squeeze 150 ml (5 fl oz) more orange and tangerine juice, warm it and add. Work to a smooth dough, adding more water and warm juice if necessary. Put the dough into an oiled bowl, cover with a cloth and leave to rise in a warm place until almost doubled in size – about an hour.

Punch the dough down in the bowl. Combine the drained currants and sultanas with the semolina flour and spice mixture and, working with your hands, combine with the dough. Turn the dough out onto a floured surface and knead for 10 minutes, adding more flour if it is sticky.

Divide the dough into three equal pieces. Oil 3 bread tins, each 1.5 litre (2½ pt) capacity. Shape each piece to fit the length of the tin and fit them in, so the corners are well filled. Cover with a cloth and leave to rise in a warm place until almost double in size – another hour.

Bake in an oven preheated to 180°C (350°F, gas 4) for 1 hour 10 minutes or more: the loaves should be a rich brown colour and make a hollow sound when the turned out bread is thumped on the bottom. Leave on a rack to cool. The bread will keep for at least 3 weeks.

BOBÓTA

COUNTRY CORN CAKE WITH COGNAC, CURRANTS AND PINE NUTS

The name of this cake is connected to the ancient Elysian rites of the grain goddess, Demeter, or Baubo, as she was sometimes known in the form of an old woman. It is a plain country cake soaked in syrup, remembered by many who ate it during World War II.

It is typical in the Orient to use syrup as a means of sweetening. I have been told by local Greek experts that you must either pour ice-cold syrup over a hot cake, or a hot syrup over a cold cake, if it is to be absorbed. Cold syrup is the preferred method.

MAKES 16

100 g (4 oz) currants
50 ml (2 fl oz) cognac
400 g (14 oz) coarse yellow corn meal (polenta)
100 g (4 oz) plain flour
1 teaspoon baking powder
1 teaspoon salt
125 ml (4 fl oz) mild olive oil
4 oranges, to give 250 ml (8 fl oz) juice
finely grated zest of 2 oranges
2 medium-sized eggs, separated
2 tablespoons sugar
100 g (4 oz) pine nuts

LEMON SYRUP
finely grated zest and juice of 2 lemons
2 tablespoons cognac
500 g (1 lb) sugar

Make the syrup a day ahead. Put the lemon zest and juice in a saucepan with 124 ml (4 fl oz) water. Add the sugar and bring slowly to the boil to dissolve, then boil for 10 minutes. Chill overnight, then stir in 2 tablespoons cognac. Soak the currants overnight in 50 ml (2 fl oz) cognac.

Sift the cornmeal, flour, baking powder and salt into a large mixing bowl. Heat the olive oil and pour into the flour, mixing everything thoroughly with a wooden spoon.

Make a well in the dough. Add the orange zest and 250 ml (8 fl oz) orange juice, the beaten egg yolks, and 2 tablespoons sugar and beat together, adding enough warm water to make a thickish smooth batter. Stir in the currants with the cognac and the pine nuts, until evenly incorporated. Whisk the egg whites to stiff peaks and fold into the mixture. Turn into a deep oiled baking tin, about 25 x 20 cm (10 x 8 in).

Bake in an oven preheated to 180°C (350°F, gas 4) for about 40-45 minutes until brown, when a skewer should come out clean. Cool for a few minutes and cut the cake into 16 slices or diamond shapes. Pour ice-cold syrup over it.

KARITHÓPITTA

WALNUT CAKE

This cake is common all over the Middle East. In Greece it is always referred to as 'Athenian'. Wherever it comes from, it is one of my favourites. If grinding the nuts in a food processor, do it in short pulses so the nuts don't turn oily.

SERVES 8

*350 g (12 oz) walnuts, very finely chopped
or ground
40 g (1½ oz) plain flour
1 tablespoon freshly ground cinnamon
6 medium-sized eggs, separated
250 g (8 oz) chunky marmalade,
home-made if possible
2 tablespoons orange flower water*

YOGURT AND ORANGE-FLOWER SAUCE

*3 tablespoons honey
2 teaspoons orange flower water
500 g (1 lb) thick Greek yogurt*

If you own a food processor, grind the nuts, then toss them together with the flour and cinnamon. Whisk the egg yolks until they are pale and creamy, then beat in the nut mixture, marmalade and orange flower water. Alternatively do this in a large bowl.

Whisk the egg whites until stiff. Stir a little into the nut mixture, to make it less stiff, then use a large spoon to fold the rest lightly into the nut mixture. Oil a 20 cm (8 in) push-bottom spring-release cake tin and then flour it and turn in the mixture.

Put the cake into an oven preheated to 200°C (400°F, gas 6) and immediately turn it down to 180°C (350°F, gas 4). Bake for 45-50 minutes, or until a tester inserted into the middle comes out clean. Run a knife around the edge. Cool in the tin for 15 minutes, then release and turn out onto a wire rack. Leave until cold.

To make the sauce, beat the honey and orange flower water into the yogurt with a wooden spoon. Pass a bowl of this sauce with the cake, or pour a little on each slice.

LADEN DONKEY *The narrow winding lanes of many island towns and villages make motorized transport impossible.*

ZVÍNGI

SWEET FRITTERS

Pandias remembers when street vendors handed out newspaper cones filled with hot *zvíngi* fresh from the pots of boiling olive oil on their carts. They should be eaten as quickly as possible – which they will be.

MAKES ABOUT 24

*2 tablespoons mild olive oil
salt
50 ml (2 fl oz) oúzo
225 g (7½ oz) plain flour, plus extra if needed
4 medium-sized eggs
finely grated zest of 1 lemon
450 ml (16 fl oz) mild olive oil for dunking
olive oil for deep frying
75 g (3 oz) almonds or walnuts, chopped*

SYRUP
100 g (4 oz) honey
2.5 cm (1 in) piece of cinnamon bark
1 clove
juice of 1 lemon

Start by making the syrup. Put the honey, cinnamon, clove and 250 ml (8 fl oz) water in a saucepan and boil until the syrup just coats the back of a wooden spoon – about 5-6 minutes. Add the lemon juice and boil for 2-3 minutes more. Chill, when it will thicken.

To make the doughnut batter, bring the olive oil, salt, *ouzo* and 125 ml (4 fl oz) water to the boil, then remove from the heat. Stir in half the flour and beat until you have a thick batter. Beat the eggs with the grated lemon zest and stir into the batter with the remaining flour.

Heat the oil, at least 4 cm (1½ in) deep, in a deep-fat fryer or other pan with raised sides, to the point when the surface trembles and the oil crackles if you sprinkle a drop of water on it (stand back).

Dip a spoon into the cold olive oil, then use it to scoop up a tablespoon of batter. Push it into the hot oil with another spoon or your finger. The fritters should swell up immediately, so put in 3 or 4 at a time, and fry until they turn golden. Remove them with a slotted spoon in the order they went into the oil (judging readiness from the colour) and drain on kitchen paper. Continue till all the batter is used, keeping the doughnuts warm meanwhile.

Pour the chilled syrup over them while they are still hot, and sprinkle with chopped nuts. Serve immediately. But if you make too many to serve hot, let the extras cool, then heat the syrup and pour over them. Sprinkle with nuts and serve cold.

MOUSTOKOÚLOURA

WINE MUST COOKIES

These are old-fashioned, rough country biscuits – satisfying and not unhealthy. They are enjoyed all day long in Greece, dunked in coffee or eaten as children's snacks.

Petimézi, Greek concentrated grape syrup is also used in Italy, where it is called *vino cotto* – cooked wine. You should be able to find it under this name in Italian delicatessens.

MAKES ABOUT 24

500 g (18 oz) plain flour, plus extra for kneading
2 teaspoons bicarbonate of soda
1 tablespoon freshly ground cinnamon
1 tablespoon freshly ground cloves
50 ml (2 fl oz) mild olive oil
2 tablespoons honey
125 ml (4 fl oz) petimézi, Greek wine must syrup
(see page 13) or Italian vino cotto, or the same
amount of honey
about 4 oranges, to make 250 ml (8 fl oz) juice
freshly grated zest of ½ orange

Sift together the flour, bicarbonate of soda, cinnamon and cloves into a large bowl, making a well in the centre. In a smaller bowl beat the olive oil with the honey, *petimézi*, grated orange zest and 125 ml (4 fl oz) orange juice and pour into the well. Mix together to make a dough, adding the remaining orange juice, as necessary.

Turn out onto a floured surface and knead for about 10 minutes until the dough is smooth but still stiff. Cover with a cloth and leave to relax for 30 minutes or longer.

Break off pieces of dough, about 2 tablespoonfuls each, and roll into snakes about 1 cm (½ in) in diameter. Press the two ends together, forming oval wreaths, and place on an oiled or non-stick baking sheet. Bake in an oven preheated to 190°C (375°F, gas 5) for 10-15 minutes – until they are brown and crunchy, but not too hard.

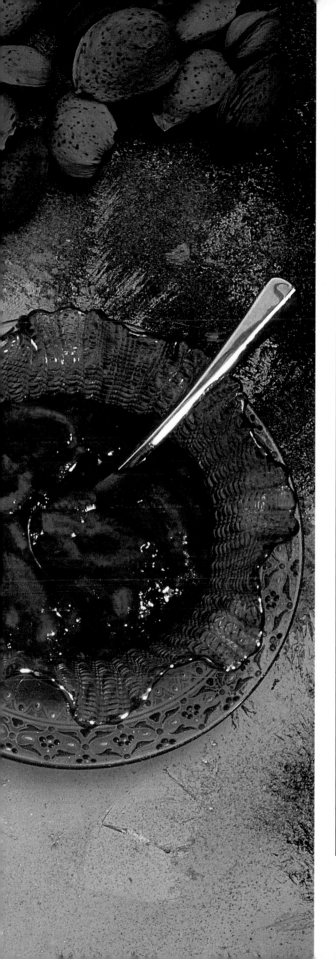

MARMELÁTHA ME LEMÓNIA

LEMON MARMALADE

In late January, early February, when the lemons glisten with pungent ripeness, I sit on the terrace wall, slicing kilos of lemons and gazing intermittently at the surrounding hills awash with almond blossoms.

MAKES 2-2.5 LITRES (3-4 PT)

2 kg (4½ lb) large, thick-skinned fresh lemons
1 teaspoon mountain thyme (see page 16)
½ teaspoon freshly picked rosemary
¼ teaspoon freshly picked oregano (see page 15)
2 tablespoons rosewater
1.8 kg (4 lb) sugar

Wash the lemons, scrubbing them well if they are waxed or siliconed from the supermarket. Cut each lemon in half lengthways from stem to tip, and slice as thinly as possible. Remove the seeds, but keep them.

Choose an enamelled or stainless steel pan big enough to hold the lemons and sugar with water, but please don't use aluminium, as the acid in the lemons will oxidize and your marmalade might turn grey. Put in the sliced lemons with any escaped juice.

Put the seeds and herbs into a cheesecloth bag and bury it in the midst of the slices. Sprinkle with 1 tablespoon rosewater and add 350 ml (12 fl oz) water. Leave to stand overnight.

The next day, bring the pot to the boil, turn it down and simmer for 1 hour. Add the sugar, stirring over low heat until it dissolves. Simmer at a very low heat, preferably with a heat diffuser underneath, for about 2 hours. You should be able to see the marmalade moving just under the surface. Test whether it is done three-quarters of the way through, then regularly, by cooling a spoonful on a saucer. When cold you can see its thickness by drawing the spoon through it. When it is thick to your liking, remove from the heat and stir in another tablespoon of rosewater.

Pour into sterilized jars, then seal. It is good immediately, better after two weeks and best after a month.

MELOMAKÁRONA ADONÍAS *left (p.138)*, MARMELÁTHA ME LEMÓNIA *right*

MELOMAKÁRONA ANDONÍAS

ANDONIA'S ANCIENT HONEY CAKES

These cakes are traditionally served at Christmas. This recipe comes from my neighbour, Andonia. I have a distinct memory of her beating the oil and sugar into the flour until it dissolved with her middle finger and forefinger as a beater – though a spoon will do.

MAKES ABOUT 4 DOZEN

1 kg (2 lb 3 oz) unbleached, plain flour, plus extra
for kneading
1½ teaspoons bicarbonate of soda
¼ teaspoon salt
400 ml (14 oz) mild olive oil
250 g (8 oz) caster sugar
125 ml (4 fl oz) cognac, mavrotháphne wine or
ruby port
finely grated zest and juice of 3 oranges
4 teaspoons freshly ground cinnamon
1½ teaspoons freshly ground clove
¾ teaspoon freshly grated nutmeg

SYRUP

500 g (1 lb) honey
250 g (8 oz) sugar
2.5 cm (1 in) piece of cinnamon bark
1 clove
finely grated zest and juice of 1 lemon

TOPPING

75 g (3 oz) almonds
1 tablespoon sugar
1 teaspoon freshly ground cinnamon

Start by making the syrup. Put the honey, sugar, cinnamon, clove and lemon zest in a saucepan and add 250 ml (8 fl oz) water. Bring to the boil and simmer 5-10 minutes. Add the lemon juice then chill.

To blanch the almonds, plunge them into boiling water for 1-2 minutes, until you see signs of their skins loosening. Then drain and slip or pop them from their skins onto a baking sheet. Toast them in an oven preheated to 180°C (350°F, gas 4) for about 10 minutes – just until they begin to colour. Cool then chop them

very, very finely – if you do this in a food processor, make sure the pulses are short, or the nuts could turn oily. Mix the ground almonds with sugar and cinnamon and reserve.

Sift the flour, bicarbonate of soda and salt together. Put the olive oil and sugar in a large bowl and beat together – with your fingers like Andonia – or with a wooden spoon. Beat in the cognac, the orange zest, spices and juice from 2 oranges – 125 ml (4 fl oz).

Then beat in the flour, a few spoonfuls at a time, until you have a malleable dough, adding more flour if it is too soft, and more orange juice if it is too stiff. Turn the dough onto a floured surface and knead for 10-15 minutes until very smooth.

Pinch off pieces of about 2 tablespoons and form into flattened oval or lozenge shapes. Place them on an oiled or non-stick baking sheet. Bake in an oven preheated to 200-215°C (400-425°F, gas 6-7) for about 20 minutes, until brown.

When they are cool enough to handle, dip them in the bowl of syrup for about 1 minute. Remove with a slotted spoon and place on a tray to cool. Sprinkle with the chopped almond mixture.

COLLECTING HONEY *The traditional sweetener of the ancient world, honey is still essential in many desserts and cakes*

PASTOKÝTHONO

QUINCE PASTE

The best quinces in the world were said to come from Cydonia in Crete, hence the name *kythóni*.

This paste is made across the entire Mediterranean. It is flavoured with lime flowers and lemon verbena, leaves usually sold for making infusions of herb tea. You may be able to find them in delicatessens among the teas. The strong flavour and good colour of the paste make it a wonderful present, packed in a box with bay leaves and greaseproof paper between the layers.

If you stop cooking the syrup at a thinner stage, you will have beautiful marmalade.

MAKES ABOUT 2½ DOZEN

3 quinces, each about 400 g (14 oz)
about 500 g (1 lb) pears
1 kg (2 lb) caster sugar, plus extra for storing
2 lemons to give about 4 tablespoons juice
40 g (1½ oz) almonds, blanched, and lightly toasted
about 2 tablespoons cognac (or poire William)

HERB INFUSION
1 tablespoon tílio, lime flowers
1 tablespoon luísa, lemon balm or lemon verbena –
about 16 leaves
6-8 leaves arbaróriza, lemon geranium leaves

A day ahead, make a strong infusion of lime flowers, lemon balm or verbena, and scented geranium leaves by putting them in a glass jar with 350 ml (12 fl oz) water and standing it in the sun all day. Alternatively, simmer them together for 15 minutes.

Peel, core and chop the quinces into chunks until you have about 1 kg (2 lb) fruit and purée in a food processor. Peel, core and chop the pears until you have 375 g (13 oz) and purée them too.

In a large heavy-bottomed pot mix the sugar with the infusion and the lemon juice. Bring slowly to the boil to dissolve the sugar, then boil for 10 minutes. Stir in the fruit pulp and bring back to the boil. Turn down the heat as low as possible – slip a heat diffuser under the pan.

Stir, cover and simmer for 2-3 hours, until the fruit turns amber-to-dark pink. Stir occasionally, to be sure the bottom is not sticking. The syrup should reduce to the consistency of a thick porridge. If this is not happening, remove the lid and continue cooking until a spoon run through the fruit leaves a trench. Be careful not to burn the bottom.

Pour the fruit pulp into a flat baking tin 30 x 30 cm (12 x 12 in) to the depth of 1½ to 2½ cm (¾-1 in). Then press the toasted almonds in at regular intervals. Cover tightly with clean cheesecloth or muslin and leave in the sun for 1 week. Or lacking Greek sun, put in an oven at its lowest heat to dry.

Brush the dried paste with cognac (I like poire William for this, but it is not a Greek product), sprinkle with sugar and cut into pieces. To store, put in an airtight box with bay leaves and greaseproof paper between the layers and eat within 6 months.

INDEX

ACKNOWLEDGMENTS

The publisher thanks the following photographers and organizations for their kind permission to reproduce the photographs in this book:

1 John Garrett/Insight; 2 La Maison de Marie Claire (Martin/ Dodeman); 3 Guy Bouchet; 6–7 Antonio Girbes; 9 Agence Top/ Pierre Putelat; 13 Explorer/Patrice Duchier; 17 Martin Breese/ Retrograph Archive; 23 Christian Sarramon; 26 27 John Garrett/Insight; 28 Pictures Colour Library/Derek Richards; 35 John Heseltine; 39 Kim Penney; 44 John Garrett/Insight; 48–49 Explorer/Paul Tatopoulos; 52–53 Robert Harding Picture Library/Lorraine Wilson; 55 Clay Perry; 58–59 Guy Bouchet; 64 Terry Harris; 70–71 John Heseltine; 75 Pix/Cornet; 80–81 Pix/ Alan Téoulé; 82–83 Campagne, Campagne/Stanislas; 89 John Garrett/Insight; 92–93 Agence Top/Pierre Putelat; 95 Antonio Girbes; 102–103 John Heseltine; 105 Antonio Girbes; 109 Jean Pierre Godeaut; 110–111 John Heseltine; 112–113 Christian Sarramon; 117 John Miller; 120 Jean Pierre Godeaut; 128 Explorer/Guy Thouvenin; 131 Agence Top/Christine Fleurent; 134 Pix/Cauchetier; 138–139 Terry Harris.

The following photographs were specially taken for Conran Octopus by Linda Burgess:
18–19, 19, 32–33, 36, 40–41, 41, 56, 60–61, 61, 66–67, 73, 76, 77, 87, 90–91, 98–99, 99, 114–115, 119, 122–123, 123, 126, 136–37.

The publishers would like to thank the following for their help with photography:
Heals, 196 Tottenham Court Road, London W1; Designer Trading, 573 King's Road, London SW6; The Greek Shop, 6 Newburgh Street, London W1; Despo and George Kouloumas.

BIBLIOGRAPHY

Apicius, *Cooking and Dining in Imperial Rome*, translated and edited by Joseph Dommers Vehling, Dover Publications Inc., 1977. (This Roman cookbook dates from the first quarter of the first millennium and bears the name of a famous gourmand of the time. It is a collection of monographs, many of which were probably originally in Greek, as the Romans esteemed all things Greek, including Greek cuisine.); Athenaeus, *The Deipnosophists* Vols I–VII, translated by Charles Burton Guleck, Heinemann Ltd, 1967. (Athenaeus (c.170–c.230AD) has the spirit of a prig, a snob and a boor, but his seven, slow-going volumes of culinary and literary hearsay are full of valuable information.); David, Elizabeth, *A Book of Mediterranean Food*, Penguin Books 1973. (Elizabeth David presented the food of the Mediterranean with knowledge and enthusiasm at a time when it might just as well have come from another planet. Mrs David is the godmother of modern Mediterranean cookbooks.); deSloover, Jacques and Goosens, Martine, *Wild Herbs, A Field Guide*, translated by Lucia Wiltd, David and Charles; Detienne, Marcel and Vernant, Jean-Pierre, *The Cuisine of Sacrifice Among Greeks*, University of Chicago Press, 1989; Durant, Will, *The Life of Greece*, Simon and Schuster, 1939; *Caesar and Christ*, Simon and Schuster, 1944; *The Age of Faith*, Simon and Schuster, 1950; Gibbons, Euell, *Stalking the Healthful Herbs*, David McKay Co., 1966. (Mr Gibbons writes about wild things with wit and wisdom. I wish his books were not out of print.); Graves, Robert, *The Greek Myths* Vols I and II, Penguin Books, 1967; Gray, Patience, *Honey From a Weed*, Prospect Books, 1986; Hale, William Harlan, *The Horizon Cookbook*, American Heritage Publishing Co. Inc., 1968; Hemphill, Rosemary, *Herbs For All Seasons*, Penguin Books, 1979; Herodotus, translated by A.D. Godley, Vols I–IV, Heinemann Ltd, 1966; Hesiod, *The Homeric Hymns and Homerica*, translated by Hugh G. Evelyn-White, 1914; Homer, *The Odyssey*, Vols I and II, translated by A.T. Murray, Heinemann Ltd, 1966; Howe, Robin, *Greek Cooking*, Mayflower Books Ltd, 1973; Kirschmann, John D. with Dunne, Lavon J., *Nutritional Almanac, Second Revised Edition*, Mcgraw-Hill, 1984; Lloyd, G.E.R., *Science, Folklore and Ideology – Studies in the Life Sciences in Ancient Greece*, Cambridge University Press, 1983; McEvedy, Colin, *The Penguin Atlas of Ancient History*, Penguin, 1982; McGee, Harild, *On Food and Cooking*, Charles Scribner's Sons, 1984. (Herein lies everything you ever wanted to know about the chemistry of cooking.); Montagne, Prosper, *The New Larousse Gastronomique*, Crown Publishers, 1977; Papoutsis, Carol, *The Festivals of Greek Easter*, D. Dsyllas, 1982; Plutarch, *Moralia*, Vol II, translated by F.C. Babitt, Heinemann Ltd.; Polunin, Oleg, *Flowers of Europe, A Field Guide*, Oxford University Press, 1969; Roden, Claudia, *A New Book of Middle Eastern Food*, Viking-Penguin Books, 1985; Root, Waverley, *Food*, Simon and Schuster, 1980. (It must have taken the better part of Waverley Root's life to compile this encyclopedia of food. It is a true labour of love, the likes of which we don't often see in these times.); Stavroulakis, Nicholas, *Cooking of the Jews of Greece*, Lycabettus Press, Athens, 1986. (Written by the curator of the Jewish museum in Athens, who took the time to collect his recipes from old people all over Greece. It is the most interesting and inspiring Greek cookbook I have ever come across.); Studola, Jiri and Lolak, Jan, edited by Sarah Bunney, *The Illustrated Book of Herbs*, Gallery Books, 1986; Stubbs, Joyce M., *The Home Book of Greek Cookery*, Faber and Faber, 1976; Tannahill, Reay, *Food in History*, Stein and Day, 1984. (The history of civilization from the standpoint of food – engrossing and well-written.); Tselemendes, Nikos, *Odygos Mageirikes*, Athens, M.I. Saliverou, 1951. (Until the first publication of this 'Cooking Guide' in 1920, there were no published cookbooks in Greece. If women were literate, they recorded their recipes in notebooks that became heirlooms. Otherwise, they passed their culinary knowledge directly to their daughters by demonstrating and telling their methods and recipes. Tselemendes, who was what we now call a caterer in Athens, is the Mrs Beeton of Greek cooking. For many people in Greece, the word for cookbook is literally "Tselemendes." Many don't even know that it was a proper name.) Wolfert, Paula, *Mediterranean Cooking*, Times Books, 1977. (I would love to be invited to this woman's house for a meal. All the recipes in all her books are mouth-watering.); Yannoulis, Anne, *Greek Calendar Cookbook*, Lucabettus Press, 1988; *The Encyclopedia Britannica*, Encyclopedia Britannica, Inc., 1970.